LET'S COOK
pasta

LET'S COOK

pasta

how to make it, cook it, serve and eat it

JENI WRIGHT

southwater

This edition is published by Southwater

Distributed in the UK by
The Manning Partnership
251–253 London Road East
Batheaston
Bath BA1 7RL
UK
tel. (0044) 01225 852 727
fax. (0044) 01225 852 852

Distributed in the USA by
Ottenheimer Publishing
5 Park Center Court
Suite 300
Owing Mills MD 2117–5001
USA
tel. (001) 410 902 9100
fax. (001) 410 902 7210

Distributed in Australia by
Sandstone Publishing
Unit 1, 360 Norton Street
Leichhardt
New South Wales 2040
Australia
tel. (0061) 2 9560 7888
fax. (0061) 2 9560 7488

Distributed in New Zealand by
Five Mile Press NZ
PO Box 33–1071
Takapuna
Auckland 9
New Zealand
tel. (0064) 9 4444 144
fax. (0064) 9 4444 518

Southwater is an imprint of Anness Publishing Limited
© 1999, 2000 Anness Publishing Limited

1 3 5 7 9 10 8 6 4 2

PUBLISHER: Joanna Lorenz
EXECUTIVE EDITOR: Linda Fraser
EDITOR: Susannah Blake
DESIGNER: Patrick McLeavey
PHOTOGRAPHERS: Janine Hosegood and William Lingwood (recipes)
FOOD FOR PHOTOGRAPHY: Annabel Ford (techniques) and Lucy McKelvie and Kate Jay (recipes)
EDITORIAL READER: Diane Ashmore
PRODUCTION CONTROLLER: Yolande Denny

Previously published as part of a larger compendium *The Pasta Bible*

CONTENTS

Introduction   6

Dried Pasta   12

Fresh Pasta   26

Equipment   32

How to Cook and Serve Pasta   36

How to Make Pasta   42

The Pasta Pantry   54

Pasta Recipes   64

Pasta Sauces   66

Quick and Healthy Pasta Dishes   76

Vegetarian Meals   86

Lunch and Supper Dishes   100

Baked Pasta Dishes   112

Index   126

Introduction

Pasta is one of the most popular foods in the world today. Available in an amazing range of shapes and flavors, it is incredibly versatile, and can be served in countless different ways. Students love it for the energy it gives them at low cost, chefs delight in introducing light and healthy sauces for modern palates, families favor casseroles that can be cooked in advance and that will stretch to serve extra guests. Simple or sophisticated, quick and easy to cook, it is the perfect choice for everyday and spur-of-the-moment meals.

Introduction

The origin of pasta

There is a great deal of controversy surrounding the origin of pasta. Who invented it? Was it the Chinese, the Italians or the Arabs? There is absolutely no doubt that Marco Polo brought noodles back to Italy from China in 1295, but most food historians agree that a kind of pasta was well-known in Italy long before this time. Wall paintings in an Etruscan tomb show utensils—a pastry board, rolling pin and wheel—that are remarkably similar to those used today for making pasta. There is also evidence that the Romans made an unleavened dough of flour and water, which they cut into pasta-like strips, fried and ate with a sauce. Apicius, the famous Roman gastronome of the 1st century A.D., described baked dishes in which a pasta-like dough was layered with other ingredients. A kind of Roman lasagne?

Wherever or whenever pasta was first "invented," it seems to have been the Sicilians who were the first to boil it in water. They learned irrigation and cultivation from the Arabs who conquered the island in the 9th century, and by the 12th century there is evidence they were eating a long thin type of pasta like spaghetti. Meanwhile, the Calabrians had mastered the art of twisting pasta strips to make tubes that resembled modern-day macaroni.

In a 13th-century Italian cookbook published just before Marco Polo's return from China, there are recipes for making different pasta shapes, including ravioli, vermicelli and tortelli. So one way or another, pasta did exist in Italy before Marco Polo, and the pasta museum in Rome has many writings, paintings and etchings to substantiate this.

By the time of the Renaissance, pasta featured frequently on Italian menus. The rich Florentines teamed it with costly sugar and spices, but the less well-off had to content themselves with eating pasta plain or with humble ingredients such as garlic, vegetables and cheese.

In those early days, pasta was simple, fresh and handmade, a far cry from the many different commercially produced dried shapes and flavors that we know today. The credit for inventing these must go to the Neapolitans.

The fertile soil in the region around Naples was found to be ideal for growing durum wheat, which makes the best flour for commercial pasta, and the unique combination of sun and wind in this part of southern Italy was just right for drying out the shapes. Once the Neapolitans discovered this, the pasta-making industry burgeoned around the city of Naples, and by the late 18th century the consumption of pasta in Italy had really taken off. Maccheroni, spaghetti and tagliatelle were among the first shapes to be produced commercially, made with flour and water only.

At this time pasta was generally regarded as food for the poor, and tended to be served with tomato sauces. Tomatoes loved the growing conditions in the south as much as the durum wheat, and once the Italians fell in love with the tomato there was no going back.

The egg-enriched pasta that northern Italians favored was not produced commercially at this time. *Pasta all'uovo* was

There is no doubt that Marco Polo brought back noodles to Italy from China in the late 13th century. However, an Italian cookbook, which was published just before his return, includes recipes for making pasta. His departure from Venice is depicted in this early 14th-century painting, Romance of Alexander.

Workers in the fields at Pitti Palace, Florence, in the late 19th century tending the hard durum wheat, which Italians call grano duro. This type of wheat produces the ideal pasta flour.

freshly made, often with a meat filling or sauce, and was served to the rich. It was not until the 20th century that improvements in industrial equipment made the manufacture of egg pasta a viable commercial proposition.

Pasta today

Wherever Italians went, they took their pasta with them. Those that emigrated to America and Great Britain adapted pasta shapes and sauces to suit local tastes and ingredients, a tradition that happily continues to this day.

Pasta is becoming more and more popular as a healthy, quick-cooking and versatile food, and Italian manufacturers have quickly responded to the demand, constantly developing new flavors and using the latest technology to create original shapes.

Commercially produced dried pasta has always been highly regarded in Italy. It is in no way inferior to fresh homemade pasta, but is simply a different form of this fabulous food. Italian cooks always keep a few packages of dried pasta in their pantries and use it on a daily basis—even in the north of Italy, where the tradition of always making fresh pasta at home endured for a lot longer than it did in the south of the country.

The right kind of wheat

The ideal variety of wheat for the flour used in commercial pasta making is durum (Triticum durum), which Italians call *grano duro*. This hard summer wheat produces a flour that is high in gluten. Dough made from durum wheat flour is pliable and easy to knead and shape. The majority of durum

wheat for the Italian pasta-making industry is grown in Italy or imported from North America. The flour from durum wheat, called *semola* in Italian, makes a high quality pasta that holds its shape well. Cooked properly until *al dente*; it should be just tender, with a pleasant nutty bite. When you are buying pasta in packages or boxes, always check that it is made from 100 percent durum wheat. The Italian phrase to look for is *pasta di semola di grano duro*. This type of pasta may be more expensive than one made with a mixture of durum wheat and soft wheat, but you will get a much better result. Inexpensive pasta made with soft wheat flour tends to stick together during cooking and its texture is often soft and flabby. Generally speaking, the Italian brands are the best. Ask the staff at your local market which brands they recommend, and spend as much as you can afford. There is a big difference in texture and taste between the higher priced Italian brands and the cheaper types of pasta, and you will quickly find that it pays to buy the best.

The northern preference for egg pasta

In southern Italy the majority of pasta is made with durum wheat and water only, and literally hundreds—if not thousands—of different shapes are manufactured. In northern Italy, the preference is for pasta with added egg, pasta all'uovo. The tradition for using this type of pasta began in Emilia, where filled and stuffed pasta shapes originated. Home cooks found that adding a little egg to the dough strengthened it and helped to keep the filling in during cooking. As Italian housewives began

Above: Healthy ingredients, such as olive oil, tomatoes, garlic and bell peppers, combine wonderfully well with pasta and are used over and over again by Italian cooks. This may be one of the reasons that the incidence of heart disease in Italy is one of the lowest in the world.

Below: The various sizes and shapes of holes in these commercial pasta dies allow for the production of a wide range of long and short pasta shapes.

Above right: In modern pasta factories sophisticated machines are used to weigh and pack the finished product.

to make less and less fresh pasta at home and started to buying it at stores, small factories started making dried egg pasta to meet the demand. Now it is fast becoming a huge industry, although there are fewer fancy shapes made with egg than there are with plain pasta. This is because egg pasta is more difficult to work with. It is not used for making long thin shapes like spaghetti because they would break too easily. Commercially manufactured *pasta all'uovo* may contain as many as 7 eggs to 2 1/4 pounds flour, so it has a richer taste than plain pasta and absorbs more water.

If you buy Italian egg pasta, the package should state that it is 100 percent durum wheat and egg *(semola di grano duro e uova)*. *Pasta all'uovo* complements the cream and butter sauces that are popular in the north. The tomato and olive oil sauces of the south have always been traditionally served with plain pasta, although pasta all'uovo is now catching on in the south, too.

The nutritional value of pasta

Rich in protein, vitamins and minerals, pasta is a complex carbohydrate food. It provides as much energy as a pure protein like steak, but with little or no fat. Of the eight amino acids essential to make up a complete protein, pasta contains six, so it only needs a small amount of cheese, meat, fish, pulses or eggs—the traditional ingredients for serving with pasta—to make it complete. If you are using *pasta all'uovo*, you need even less additional protein.

The key to healthy eating lies in eating pasta as the Italians do, with only a small amount of extra ingredients. In Italy, it is traditional for pasta to be served as a first course, before the main course of fish or meat. Eaten with a small spoonful of sauce and a light sprinkling of grated cheese, nothing could be more well-balanced and nutritionally sound.

The incidence of heart disease in Italy is one of the lowest in the world, and doctors, nutritionists and scientists agree that the Italian diet plays a large and important role in this. In Italian cooking, healthy ingredients, such as extra virgin olive oil, fresh and canned tomatoes, garlic, onions, olives, red bell peppers and fresh parsley are used all the time, plus lots of fresh fish, vegetables and salad leaves, fruit, pulses and lemon juice. Most of these ingredients combine wonderfully well with pasta, and they are used over and over again in the recipes in this book.

Pasta is a completely natural food that contains no additives. Pasta with egg contains the most nutrients, while whole-wheat pasta has the highest percentage of vitamins and fiber. Always check the label when buying colored pasta, because some varieties include artificial coloring.

Pasta is inexpensive, quick and easy to cook, and incredibly versatile. It is the perfect convenience food: in the time it takes to boil the water and cook the pasta, most sauces are ready to serve. Pasta all'uovo is especially nutritious and good for children who don't like eggs in a more recognizable form. Another plus, which athletes appreciate, is that as a high-energy food, pasta is easy to digest and yet immensely satisfying.

It makes sense, therefore, to include pasta in our diets as often as possible, if not every day. Since everybody loves it, this should be very easy to do. People watching their weight may be surprised to know that a 3-ounce portion of cooked pasta yields only about 100 calories and can therefore be eaten as part of a calorie-controlled diet, as long as it is only lightly sauced.

Pasta as an everyday meal

In Italy, pasta is generally eaten as a first course (*primo piatto* or just *primo*) as part of the main meal of the day. This may be at lunchtime or in the evening, depending on family circumstances and whether the meal is served during the week or on the weekend. The meal usually begins with antipasto, which is followed by a *primo piatto* of either soup, pasta, rice or gnocchi. Pasta used to be served as a lunchtime first course when lunch was traditionally the main meal of the day, but now that more and more Italian women are working outside the home, these customs are changing and there are fewer hard-and-fast rules about lunch and dinner. After the *primo piatto*, the second course, *secondo piatto*, is served. This is either fish or meat followed by vegetables or salad, then cheese, fresh fruit and coffee. Desserts are normally reserved for special occasions.

When pasta is served as a first course, the usual amount is $2^{1}/2$–$3^{1}/2$ ounces uncooked weight per person. Sauce is added sparingly, tossed with the freshly drained hot pasta in the kitchen, and the mixture is then brought to the table in one large bowl. By the time the pasta

Colored pasta looks and tastes very good, but always check the label before buying, because some varieties include artificial coloring.

reaches the dining room it has mingled with the sauce and taken on some of its flavor. In some homes the bowl is passed around the table and everyone helps themselves, while in others one person does the serving. When you are serving pasta directly from the bowl, it looks most attractive if you retain a small ladleful of the sauce to put on top of the pasta after tossing, then sprinkle with cheese or herbs at the last moment.

If it suits your lifestyle best to serve pasta as a main course for lunch or supper, simply increase the weight of uncooked pasta to 4–6 ounces per person and make more sauce. For convenience, you may prefer to serve pasta in shallow soup plates or bowls or on dinner plates. Warm these beforehand and serve and eat the pasta as soon as possible so that it can be enjoyed at its best. If you accompany your main course with a fresh green salad and follow with some fresh fruit, you will have a tasty, nutritious and supremely satisfying meal. *Buon Appetito!*

Although traditionally served from one large bowl that is passed around the table, you may prefer to serve pasta in shallow individual soup plates or bowls.

Dried Pasta

The many hundreds of different types of dried pasta are divided into categories. Long, short and flat shapes are the most common, but there are also stuffed shapes, shapes suitable for stuffing and tiny shapes for use in soup. Among these, you will find some less well-known regional shapes and the more unusual and decorative designer shapes.

Only buy dried pasta that is made using 100 percent durum wheat. If you decant pasta shapes into storage jars, use up any remaining pasta before adding more from a new package. Older pasta may take longer to cook than that from a fresher package, and different brands of the same shape may not necessarily require the same cooking time.

LONG PASTA / *PASTA LUNGA*

Dried long pasta in the form of spaghetti is probably the best-known pasta of all time, and was certainly one of the first types to be exported from Italy. Spaghetti is still very widely used, but nowadays there are many other varieties of long pasta that look and taste just as good. There are no hard-and-fast rules when matching pasta to sauce, so experiment with alternative varieties to add interest to your cooking, always remembering that long pasta is best served with either a thin, rich sauce or one that is smooth and thick. If too thin and watery, the sauce will simply run off the long strands; if too chunky or heavy, the sauce will fall to the bottom of the bowl and you will be left with a bowl full of chunks and no pasta to eat it with. Rich sauces made with olive oil, butter, cream, eggs, finely grated cheese and chopped fresh herbs are good with long pasta. When ingredients such as vegetables, fish and meat are added to a smooth thick sauce, they should be very finely chopped.

Long pasta comes in different lengths, but 12 inches is about the average. In specialty food stores, you may see dried pasta that is much longer than this, but think twice before buying it because extra-long pasta can be tricky to cook and eat and often not worth the bother. The width of long pasta varies too; the strands can be flat, hollow, round or square, while other types have the pasta strands coiled up into nests.

Most long shapes are available in plain durum wheat only. The shapes made with egg (*all'uovo*) are very delicate, and are either packed in nests or compressed as waves. Fine long pasta, such as spaghetti, is far too delicate to be made with egg, but a short version from Emilia-Romagna, called *capricciosa all'uovo*, is available.

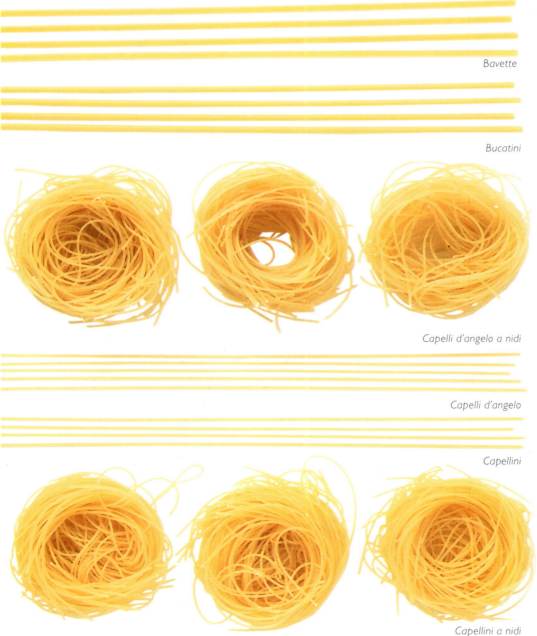

Bavette

Bucatini

Capelli d'angelo a nidi

Capelli d'angelo

Capellini

Capellini a nidi

Bavette

This type of long pasta is known all over Italy, but is very common in the South. The noodles are narrow and flat, like tagliatelle, only slimmer. Indeed, some southern Italians use the name bavette to describe tagliatelle. Bavettine is a narrower version. Both types can be plain or *all'uovo* (with egg).

Bucatini

This looks like spaghetti but is slightly chunkier. The strands are hollow (*buco* means hole), like hard, inflexible drinking straws. This type of pasta is best known in the Roman dish, *Bucatini all'Amatriciana*, which has a tomato, bacon and pepper sauce, and in Sicily it is traditionally served with a sauce of fresh sardines. Bucatoni is a fatter version, while perciatelli is bucatini by another name.

Capelli d'angelo

The name means angel's hair, which is an evocative description for this extremely fine pasta. It is used in broths and soups, and is popular with children. You may find it packed in nests, labeled capelli d'angelo a nidi. These nests are easy to handle and cook—one nest per person is the usual serving, so you can use as many nests as you need. Capellini and capel Venere are similar to capelli d'angelo.

Chitarra

Also known as spaghetti alla chitarra, this type of pasta is cut on a special wooden frame strung with wires like guitar strings (*chitarra* is Italian for guitar). It is therefore square-shaped rather than round, but can be used as an alternative to spaghetti.

Fusilli

Spaghetti spirals that look like long opened-out corkscrews. You may see these labeled fusilli lunghi or fusilli col buco, to distinguish them from the more widely known short fusilli and eliche. Fusilli is often used with tomato sauces.

Lasagnette

This flat pasta resembles tagliatelle, but the noodles are slightly wider. There are several types, most of which have frilly edges. Reginette is similar. You can use lasagnette in place of any ribbon pasta.

Linguine

In Italian, the name means little tongues and accurately describes a very thin spaghetti-like pasta that has flattened edges. You may also see linguinette and lingue di passera (sparrows' tongues), both of which are even narrower. Whole-wheat linguine is also available. All are good with the simple olive oil-based sauces and smooth tomato sauces of southern Italy.

Maccheroni

A very familiar form of pasta. We know a short version of it as macaroni, but in Italy the long thick tubes are widely used for all kinds of sauces—in some regions the word maccheroni is even used as a generic term for pasta and maccheroncini, is simply the name given to very thin, long pasta. Maccheroni comes in different lengths and thicknesses, with straight or angled ends, in plain, egg and whole-wheat varieties. There is even a square-shaped chitarra version, which comes from Abruzzi. There they call it maccheroni alla chitarra, but it also goes by the name of tonnarelli. Maccheroni is useful because it goes with so many different sauces.

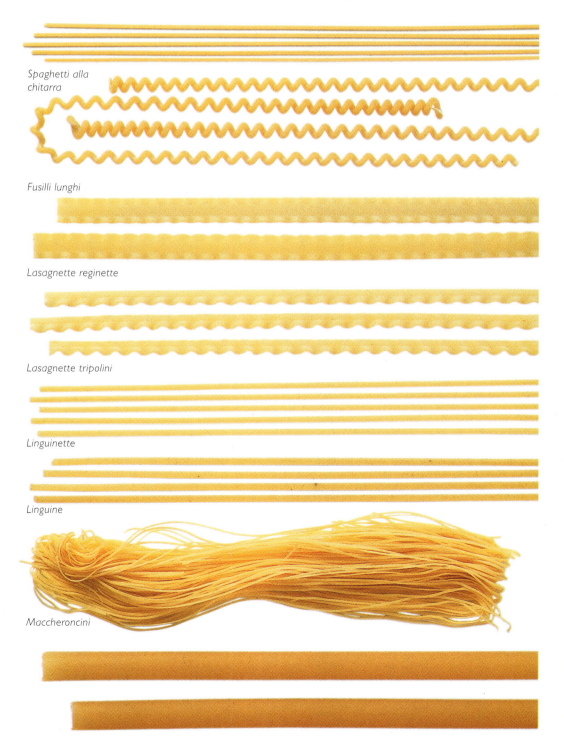

Spaghetti alla chitarra

Fusilli lunghi

Lasagnette reginette

Lasagnette tripolini

Linguinette

Linguine

Maccheroncini

Maccheroni

Spaghetti

This familiar type of pasta takes its name from the word *spago*, which means string. Spaghetti means little strings; spaghettini is a thinner variety, and spaghettoni is thicker. Spaghetti originally came from Naples, but today it is made in other parts of Italy too, and the length and width vary from one region to another.

Numerous different brands, flavors and colors are available, including whole-wheat (*integrali*), spinach (*spinaci*) and chile (*peperoncini*) so the choice is yours, but avoid the inexpensive brands. Long Italian spaghetti tends to be very good; it is graded by number according to the thickness. Good-quality spaghetti made in Italy is still one of the best forms of pasta, despite the ever-increasing range of other shapes. It goes well with many different kinds of sauces.

Tagliatelle

The most common form of ribbon noodles, tagliatelle derives its name from the Italian verb *tagliare* meaning to cut. The noodles are usually about $1/3$–$1/2$ inch wide, but there are fine versions called tagliatellina, tagliarini and tagliolini, and an even finer type called tagliolini fini. Traditional tagliatelle comes from Bologna. It is made both with and without egg and with spinach (*verdi*), but new flavors and colors are constantly coming into the market.

All types of tagliatelle are sold coiled in nests, which conveniently unravel during cooking when given a good stir. Paglia e fieno, which literally means straw and hay, is a mixture consisting of half plain egg and half spinach egg pasta, packed together in separate bundles of each color. The noodles are usually quite thin, either tagliarini or tagliolini. Both tagliatelle and paglia e fieno are very popular because they go well with most sauces, although strictly speaking, tagliatelle should not be served with a fish sauce. Meat sauce is the classic, as in *Tagliatelle alla Bolognese*.

The Roman version of tagliatelle is called fettuccine. These long, flat noodles are virtually the same as tagliatelle, but slightly thinner.

Spaghetti

Spaghetti integrali

Spaghetti con spinaci

Spaghettoni

Spaghettini

Spaghettini con peperoncini

Tagliatelle / tagliatelle verdi

Vermicelli

Ziti

Mezza zita

Vermicelli

This sounds appealing, but the name means little worms, which is rather unfortunate. It describes a very fine form of spaghetti—the original Neapolitan name for spaghetti was vermicelli, and southern Italians still sometimes refer to spaghetti as vermicelli, which can be confusing. This type of pasta comes in plain and egg (all'uovo) varieties and is very versatile, going well with most light sauces, but especially the light, fresh tomato and seafood sauces for which Naples is famous. There is an even finer version called vermicellini, and a similar noodle called fidelini.

Ziti

This pasta takes its name from the word zita, meaning fiancée. In the old days it was traditional in southern Italy to serve ziti at wedding feasts and on other special occasions. Ziti is very long, thick and hollow—like maccheroni—and the custom is to break it into the length desired when you cook it. Because of their size, the tubes go well with robust and chunky sauces; they are also sometimes broken into short lengths and baked in a *timballo*, which is a cup-shaped mold. The pasta is used to line the mold, which is then filled with a savory mixture such as mushrooms, ham or chicken livers combined with a sauce and topped with cheese. Zitoni are fatter than ziti; mezza zita are thinner.

Tagliolini all'uovo

Paglia e fieno

Tagliarini all'uovo

SOME REGIONAL TYPES OF LONG DRIED PASTA

Fettuccine comes from Lazio, and these noodles are used in classic Roman pasta dishes, such as *Fettuccine all'Alfredo*. They are flat ribbons, like tagliatelle but narrower (about $^1/4$ inch wide), and always sold coiled into loose nests. The three most common types are plain durum wheat, with egg (all'uovo), and with spinach (verdi), and you can use them interchangeably with tagliatelle. Fettuccelle is similar, but is straight rather than coiled. Fettuccelle integrali is the whole-wheat variety.

Frappe is a type of pasta from Emilia-Romagna. The $1–1^1/2$-inch wide noodles are flat, with wavy edges, about halfway in size between tagliatelle and lasagne. Made with egg and very delicate, the noodles are packed by a special machine that presses them into waves.

Pappardelle are broad ribbon noodles ($^3/4–1$ inch wide), with wavy edges. They come from Tuscany, where they are still made fresh with egg every day, but dried versions are now becoming more widely available, many of them with only one wavy edge or straight edges. They are good with heavy meat and game sauces. Nastroni are similar straight-sided noodles that are sold coiled into nests.

Trenette are noodles from Liguria, where they are traditionally served with pesto sauce. The Genoese dish, *Trenette alla Genovese*, combines trenette with pesto, potatoes and beans. The noodles are about $^1/8$ inch wide, and are made with egg. They resemble bavette and linguine, which can be substituted for them if trenette proves difficult to find.

Fettuccine al nero

Pappardelle

Trenette

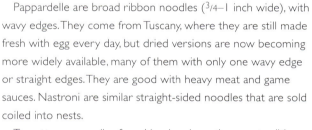

Fettuccelle

Frappe

Nastroni

SHORT PASTA / *PASTA CORTA*

There are literally hundreds of different short pasta shapes, and new ones are constantly arriving in stores. Some people prefer short pasta simply because it is easier to cook and eat than long pasta. It also goes well with many different sauces, and in most cases you can choose any shape you desire, regardless of whether your sauce is a smooth tomato-, cream- or olive oil-based type, or is chunky with large pieces of fish, meat or vegetables. Exceptions are regional dishes that are traditionally cooked with a specific shape, such as *Penne all'Arrabbiata* from Lazio.

Short pasta is divided into two main groups. Pasta secca is factory-made, using durum wheat flour and water. This is by far the largest group, and you will find that most packages of dried pasta list only these two ingredients on the label. Pasta all'uovo is made with the addition of eggs. It is naturally a brighter yellow than pasta secca and has more nutritional value. Popular in the north of Italy, especially in Emilia-Romagna, pasta all'uovo has different properties than plain pasta and goes especially well with the rich creamy and meaty sauces associated with that part of Italy. It has an advantage over plain durum wheat pasta in that it cooks slightly more quickly and is less likely to become overcooked and soggy. Although it is more expensive than plain pasta, egg pasta is becoming more popular and therefore more widely available, so look for it in an increasing number of shapes.

New flavors and colors in short pasta shapes are on the increase too. For many years, tomato (*pomodoro*) and spinach (*verdi*) were all that was available, but today there seems to be no end to the number of different color and flavor combinations, ranging from garlic, chiles and herbs to beet, salmon, mushroom, squid ink and even chocolate. Often three colors (red, white and green) are packed together and labeled tricolore. Whole-wheat pasta, called pasta integrale is made from durum wheat and other cereals. It is higher in fiber than plain durum wheat pasta and takes longer to cook. It has a chewy texture and nutty flavor.

Benfatti

Benfatti

The word *benfatti* means well made and originally described the little scraps of pasta left over from making other shapes, such as tagliatelle. Traditionally these were used in soups so they would not be wasted, but they proved so popular that they are now made and marketed as a shape in their own right. Benfatti are available plain and with egg, and are good in salads as well as soups.

Chifferini rigatini

Chifferini

Also called chifferi, chifferoni and chifferotti, these are small curved tubes like short maccheroni that has been bent. Some versions are ridged (rigatini). The holes in the middle fill with sauce, making them an excellent shape for all types of pasta sauces and soups.

Conchigliette rigate

Conchiglie

As the name suggests, these shapes resemble small conch shells. Sometimes they are ridged, in which case they are called conchiglie rigate. They are one of the most useful small shapes because they are concave and trap virtually any sauce. For this reason they are extremely popular and are widely available in many different colors

Conchiglie rigate

Conchiglioni rigati

and flavors. Sizes vary too, from tiny conchigliette for soups to conchiglione, which are jumbo shells for stuffing.

Eliche

The name comes from the Italian word for screws or propellers, which is exactly what these shapes look like. They are often mislabeled as fusilli, which are similar, but when you see the two side by side there is a marked difference. Eliche are short lengths of pasta, each twisted into a spiral, like the thread of a screw. They are available in different thicknesses, colors and flavors, including whole-wheat and tricolore, and are good with most sauces, but especially those that are tomato-based. You may only be able to buy them labeled as fusilli—the two are interchangeable and their names often depend on which part of Italy they come from.

Eliche all'uovo

Eliche tricolori

Farfalle

Farfalle verde

Farfalle salmonseppia

Farfalle tricolore

Fusilli

Fusilli con spinaci

Fusilli all'uovo

Lumache rigate

Lumachoni rigati

Gomiti rigati

Maccheroni

Maccheroncelli

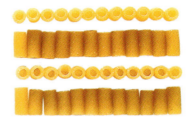

Tubetti

Farfalle

The word means butterflies, but these shapes are sometimes also described as bow-ties—the Italian word for bow-tie is *cravatta a farfalla*. They are very pretty, with crinkled edges, and are sometimes ridged. Due to their popularity, they are available in a wide variety of colors and flavors, plain, with egg and tricolore (plain, tomato and spinach flavors, which are sold together in mixed packages). Farfalle can be served with any sauce, but they are particularly good with cream and tomato sauces. Children love them. In Modena, farfalle are known as strichetti.

Fusilli

These spirals of thin pasta look like tight coils or springs and are formed by winding fresh dough around a thin rod. The spiral opens out, rather than remaining solid as it does in the case of eliche, for which fusilli are often mistaken. Check when buying, because most packages of fusilli are in fact eliche. Genuine fusilli is likely to be plain, neither made with egg nor colored. The shapes go well with thin sauces.

Lumache

Snail shells were the inspiration for this attractively shaped pasta. Unlike conchiglie, they are not shaped like conch shells, but resemble a larger version of pipe, because they are fashioned out of hollow pasta. Lumache are excellent for trapping sauces. The most common type available is lumache rigate (ridged), and there is also a large version called lumaconi. Gomiti is a similar conch shell shape.

Maccheroni

When cooks in the south of Italy speak of maccheroni, they usually mean long pasta, but in the north of the country they prefer it short. It is the short type that is generally exported as macaroni (sometimes labeled "elbow macaroni," although some brands are straighter than others). This used to be the most common short pasta shape outside Italy, but other more interesting shapes now rival it in popularity. Being hollow, it is a good shape for most sauces and baked dishes, so will always remain popular. Both plain and egg maccheroni are available, and there are also many different sizes, including a thin, quick-cooking variety. Tubetti is the name given to a miniature version that is often used in soups.

Penne lisce

Penne rigate

Penne rigate con spinaci

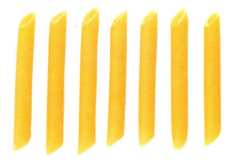

Penne mezzanine

Mezze penne tricolori

Pennoni

Penne

Like maccheroni, penne are hollow tubes, but their ends are cut diagonally so they are pointed like quills (penne means feather or quill pen). In the popularity stakes, they seem to have taken over from maccheroni, possibly because of their more interesting shape. They go well with virtually every sauce and are particularly good with chunky sauces, as their sturdiness means they hold the weight well. Penne lisce are smooth; penne rigate are ridged. Other less common varieties include the small and thin pennette and even thinner pennini and penne mezzanine, the short and stubby mezze penne or "half penne," and the large pennoni. Penne made with egg and flavored penne are very common.

Pipe rigate

Pipe

These shapes look like a cross between conchiglie and lumache. They are curved and hollow (the name means pipes) and more often than not ridged (pipe rigate). As short pasta shapes go, they are quite small. They are excellent for catching sauce and make an interesting change from other more common hollow varieties. Plain and whole-wheat types are available, and there is also a smaller version called pipette.

Rigatoni

Mezzi rigatoni

Elicoidali

Elicoidali con basilico

Rigatoni

From the maccheroni family, these are ridged, hollow, chunky-looking shapes. They are very popular because they are sturdy enough to hold chunky sauces, and they come in many flavors. There is a short version called mezzi rigatoni and a straight, stubby version called millerighe. The texture of rigatoni always seems slightly chewier than that of other short pasta. Similar in shape but slightly narrower are elicoidali, which have curved ridges (their name means helixes). Elicoidali can be plain or flavored with ingredients such as basil.

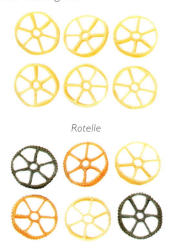

Rotelle

Rotelle tricolore

Rotelle

These are cartwheel shapes. There is a ridged variety, rotelle rigate, and sometimes this shape goes by other names, such as ruote, ruote di carro and trulli. Although not a classic Italian shape, the spokes of the wheels are very good for holding chunky sauces. Children like them, and most supermarkets sell them in different colors and flavors. The plain Italian brands taste very good.

SOME REGIONAL TYPES OF SHORT DRIED PASTA

Garganelli come from Emilia-Romagna. They are tubular egg pasta shapes that resemble penne, but look more like scrolls than quills because you can clearly see how they have been rolled. This is done on a special tool, called *il pettine*, that looks like a large comb.

Gnocchi sardi are from Sardinia. They are named after the gnocchi potato dumplings, but are smaller, like little razor shells. Gnocchetti sardi are smaller still, and are mostly used in soups. Malloreddus is another Sardinian name for gnocchi. These shapes are often flavored with saffron and served with traditional meat and vegetable sauces. They are quite chewy in texture.

Orecchiette, or little ears, are from Puglia in the south-east of Italy. Always made with durum wheat, they have a chewy texture and are served with the traditional sauces of the region, especially those made with broccoli.

Pizzoccheri are buckwheat noodles from Valtellina in Lombardy, not far from the border with Switzerland. They are thin and flat and usually sold in nests (*a nidi*) like fettuccine, but they are about half the length. Pizzoccheri are also sometimes cut to make short noodles. Their flavor is nutty, and they go well with the robust flavors of northern Italian cuisine, most famously with cabbage, potatoes and cheese in the baked dish of the same name.

Strozzapreti, which literally translated means priest stranglers, come from Modena. They are said to derive their name from the story of a priest who liked them so much he ate too many—and nearly choked to death. In fact, strozzapreti consist of two pieces of pasta twisted or "strangled" together. Other similar twisted shapes are caserecce, fileia and gemelli. The Genoese trofie, although not twisted, are similar, and can be substituted for strozzapreti.

Trofie are from the Ligurian port of Genoa, where it is traditional to serve them with pesto sauce. They are rolls of solid pasta with pointed ends, quite small and dainty. At one time you could only get homemade trofie, but now they are available dried at Italian specialty stores, in which case the shapes are sometimes open along one side rather than solid. They are well worth buying if you want to make an authentic *Genoese Trofie al Pesto*.

Above from the top: Garganelli all'uovo, garganelli paglia e fieno, girondole di Puglia, gnocchi sardi integrali and gnocchetti sardi

Gnocchetti sardi

Pizzocheri a nidi

Strozzapreti

Orecchiette

Short-cut pizzocheri

Trofie

FLAT PASTA

Although there are many kinds of long flat ribbon pasta, such as fettuccine and tagliatelle, there is really only one broad, flat pasta used for baking in the oven (*al forno*), and that is lasagne. Thin sheets of lasagne are designed to be baked between layers of sauce in the oven, or cooked in boiling water until *al dente*, rolled around a filling to make cannelloni, then baked. All types of lasagne are designed to be used in this way, and are never served with a separate sauce.

Plain lasagne

Made from durum wheat and water, this type of lasagne comes flat-packed in boxes. There are three different colors—yellow (plain), green (*verdi*), which is made with spinach, and brown or wholewheat (*integrali*). The shape varies according to the manufacturer, from narrow or broad rectangles to squares. Most sheets are completely flat, but some are wavy all over. Others have crimped or curly edges, which help to trap the sauce and look attractive too. Get to know the different brands and their sizes and choose the ones that fit your baking dish, to avoid having to cut them to fit. This makes light work of assembling the layers before baking. Check the cooking instructions on the box because regular plain lasagne needs to be pre-cooked before being layered or rolled. The usual method is to plunge about four sheets at a time into a large pan of salted boiling water, boil for about 8 minutes until *al dente*, then carefully remove each sheet with a large slotted spoon and/or tongs and lay it flat on a damp cloth to drain. The sheets need to be drained in a single layer or they will stick to each other. This method is fairly time-consuming and messy, but once it has been completed and the lasagne has been assembled, the cooking time is usually only about 30 minutes.

Lasagnette are long, narrow strips of flat pasta, which are crimped on one or two sides. They are used in the same way as lasagne, layered with sauces, then topped with grated cheese and baked. Festonelle are small squares of lasagnette, which are also used in baked dishes.

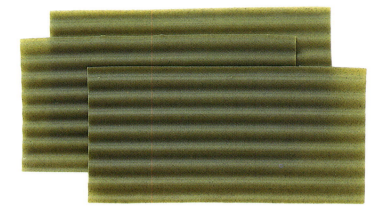

Lasagne verdi

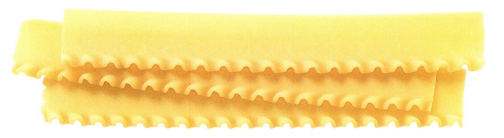

Lasagnette

Lasagnette

Festonelle

Pantacce

Lasagne

Lasagne

Lasagne verdi

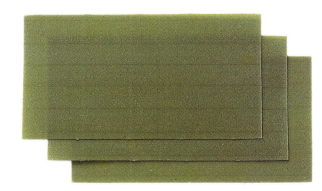

Lasagne verdi all'uovo

Pantacce are tiny diagonal pieces cut from lasagnette. They are similar to the hand-cut quadrucci and can be used in baked dishes, but are more often added to soups.

Lasagne all'uovo

This type of lasagne is made with durum wheat and water like plain lasagne, but with the addition of egg. This makes it a brighter yellow than plain lasagne, and richer in flavor and nutrients. It is available as plain egg (lasagne all'uovo) and egg and spinach (lasagne verdi all'uovo). Like the plain lasagne, it comes in different shapes and sizes with a variety of different edgings.

Lasagne

Lasagne all'uovo

Easy-cook lasagne

Although a relatively recent innovation, easy-cook lasagne is fast becoming the number one favorite. Sometimes labeled "no pre-cooking required," it does not need to be boiled first, but is layered in the baking dish straight from the package, so saving lots of time and mess. As with the plain and egg lasagne, it comes in all sorts of different shapes, sizes and colors, with straight or fancy edges. It is easiest to use if it is the right shape to fit neatly into your baking dish, although it can be broken to fit. Baking time is slightly longer than with the pre-boiled varieties, so allow at least 40 minutes. Make sure that the sauce you use is runnier than usual because this type of lasagne absorbs liquid during baking and needs extra sauce to stay moist.

Tortellini all'uovo

Tortellini verdi

Ravioli all'uovo

Agnolotti all'uovo

DRIED STUFFED PASTA

The most common dried stuffed pasta shapes are tortellini (little pies), a specialty of Bologna said to be modeled on the shape of Venus's navel. They are made from rounds or circles, of pasta, so they look like little plump rings, another name for them is anolini. Some Italian specialty stores also sell dried cappelletti (little hats), which resemble tortellini but are made from squares of pasta and have little peaks. Cappelletti are more likely to be sold fresh than dried. The same goes for ravioli and agnolotti, although you will find them frozen at most supermarkets. Tortellini are popular dried because they are traditionally used *in brodo*—simmered in a clear beef or chicken stock until they swell and plump up to make a satisfying soup. Most

Italian cooks keep a package or two of tortellini in the pantry for just this purpose, and *Tortellini in Brodo* is often served for an evening meal when the main meal of the day has been at lunchtime. You can also be sure that *Tortellini in Brodo* will be served as a pick-me-up if ever a member of the family is unwell. They are also traditionally served on New Year's Eve in Bologna, perhaps as an antidote to the excesses of Christmas.

Dried tortellini are generally available with a choice of fillings—with meat (*alla carne*) or cheese (*ai formaggi*). The pasta is made with egg and may be plain and yellow in color, green if flavored with spinach, or red if flavored with tomato. All types of tortellini need to be cooked for at least 15 minutes to allow time for the pasta to swell and the ingredients in the filling to plump up and develop their flavor. Meat fillings are a mixture of pork sausage and beef with bread crumbs, Parmesan cheese and spices. Cheese fillings usually consist of a minimum of 35 percent cheese mixed with bread crumbs and spices.

Dried tortellini are a useful pantry item as they will keep for up to 12 months (but always check the use-by date on the package). For a soup, only a handful or two of the filled shapes are needed and the package can be resealed. Tortellini are also good boiled, then drained and tossed in melted butter and herbs or a cream, tomato or meat sauce, and served with grated Parmesan. Children like their shape, and they provide a good way of persuading them to eat meat and cheese. A 9-ounce package will serve four people.

DRIED PASTA FOR STUFFING

Large pasta shapes are made commercially for stuffing and baking in the oven. Fillings vary, from meat and poultry to spinach, mushrooms and cheese, and the pasta can be baked in either a béchamel or a tomato sauce. Keep the filling moist and the sauce runny to ensure that the finished dish will not be dry. Dried shapes make an interesting change from lasagne, especially for children's meals, and they are attractive as a first course for a dinner party. They do not need to be boiled before being stuffed.

Cannelloni

Cannelloni

These large pasta tubes (their name means large reeds) are about 4 inches long. Plain, spinach and whole-wheat versions are available. In Italy, cannelloni is traditionally made from fresh sheets of lasagne rolled around a filling, but the ready-made dried tubes are convenient and less time-consuming to use. They are easy to stuff, using either a teaspoon or a piping bag.

Conchiglie

Conchiglie

Sometimes also called conchiglioni, these jumbo conch shells are available in plain, spinach and tomato flavors, both smooth and ridged. There are often two sizes—medium and large—both of which are suitable for stuffing, although you will probably find the larger ones less difficult.

Lumaconi

Lumaconi

These are like conchiglie, but are elbow-shaped—like large snail shells—with an opening at either end. The ones most commonly available are plain and ridged, but you may find different colors in specialty stores. You may also come across similar shapes called chioccioloni, gorzettoni, manicotti and tuffolini.

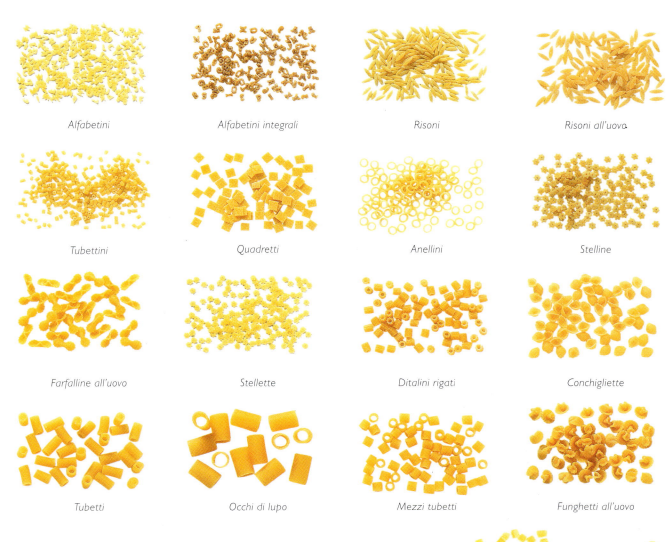

Alfabetini	*Alfabetini integrali*	*Risoni*	*Risoni all'uova*
Tubettini	*Quadretti*	*Anellini*	*Stelline*
Farfalline all'uovo	*Stellette*	*Ditalini rigati*	*Conchigliette*
Tubetti	*Occhi di lupo*	*Mezzi tubetti*	*Funghetti all'uovo*

DRIED PASTA FOR SOUP / *PASTINA*

Teeny-weeny pasta shapes are called pastina in Italian, and there are literally hundreds of different ones to choose from. They are mostly made from plain durum wheat, although you may find them with egg and even flavored with carrot or spinach. In Italy, they are always served in broths and clear soups, and are regarded almost as nursery food because they are so often served for children's meals (many Italian babies are weaned on them) or as a pick-me-up for adults who are not feeling well. If you stay in an Italian hospital, you are likely to be served *Pastina in Brodo*.

Shapes of pastina vary enormously, and seem to get more and more fanciful as the market demands.

The smallest and most plain *pasta per minestre* (pasta for soups) are like tiny grains. Some look like rice and are in fact called risi or risoni, while others are more like barley and are called orzi. Fregola, from Sardinia, look like couscous, and have a similar nutty texture and flavor. Semi di melone are like melon seeds, as their name suggests, while acini de pepe or peperini are named after peppercorns, which they resemble in shape and size if not in color. Coralline, grattini and occhi are three more very popular tiny shapes.

The next size up are the ones that are most popular with children. These include alfabeti and alfabetini (alphabet shapes), stelline and stellette (stars), rotellini (tiny wagon wheels) and anellini, which can be tiny rings, sometimes with ridges that make them look very pretty, or larger hoops. Ditali are similar to anellini but slightly thicker, while tubettini are thicker still.

Another category of pasta per minestre consists of slightly larger shapes, more like miniature versions of familiar types of short pasta. Their names end in "ine," "ette" or "etti," denoting that they are the diminutive forms. These include conchigliette (little shells), farfalline and farfallette (little bows), funghetti (little mushrooms), lumachine

Peperini

(little snails), quadretti and quadrettini (little squares), orecchiettini (little ears), renette (like baby penne) and tubetti (little tubes). The size of these varies: the smaller ones are for use in clear broths, while the larger ones are more often used in thicker soups, such as minestrone.

Designer Pasta

Relative newcomers to the market are the pasta shapes that bear little or no resemblance to the traditional or regional Italian varieties. Many of these are made outside Italy in any case, while the ones made in Italy are often for export only. It seems that the majority of Italians are happy enough with the pasta they know and love.

Supermarkets and food halls, gourmet stores and specialty stores are the best places to find these new shapes. Quality varies enormously, and some of them are nothing more than a gimmick, with very disappointing textures and flavors. Others are more successful, especially the ones made by long-established Italian firms. They are a nice change from the more common shapes and are often an interesting conversation piece, especially when you are entertaining. As a general rule, flavored pasta is best served with very simple sauces based on olive oil or butter, otherwise the flavors of the pasta and sauce tend to cancel each other out.

LONG SHAPES AND NOODLES

Spaghetti and tagliatelle are often flavored and colored. These shapes are either dramatically long or coiled in nests (*a nidi*), and you can even buy a type of pasta called spagliatelle, which is like a cross between the two. You can choose from a single flavor in one package, or up to five different flavors combined, and they can be either plain durum wheat pasta or made with the addition of egg and labeled "*all'uovo*". Spinach, tomato, mushroom, beet, saffron and smoked salmon are all popular flavors, but there are also other stronger flavors, such as chile and garlic (singly and together) and black squid ink (*nero di seppia*). One of the most fanciful

Tagliatelle flavored with red and green chiles

Egg and smoked salmon-flavored tagliatelle

Three-color tagliatelle

Porcini-flavored tagliatelle

Tagliatelle flavored with squid ink and bottarga (mullet roe)

Garlic- and chile-flavored spaghetti

Porcini-flavored tagliatelle

Poppy seed tagliatelle

Porcini-flavored bavette

Five-color spagliatelle

Multicolored arlecchino

Basil-flavored strangozzi

combinations comes from Venice. Called arlecchino (harlequin), it is a mixture of black (squid ink), green (spinach and herbs), red (tomato and beet) and blue (blueberry and blue Curaçao liqueur). More common and perhaps most successful is tagliatelle speckled with herbs or seeds or, if it comes from Tuscany, flavored with wild mushrooms (porcini). A broad variety of tagliatelle called bavette from Puglia is also flavored with porcini. Strangozzi is an unusual thin noodle from Umbria. It comes plain and flavored with spinach, basil, spinach and basil, or tomato. It is sometimes sold twisted into a long, thick braid, which looks pretty in the package but is best broken into short lengths to cook.

Short Shapes

The most inventive and unusual designer shapes fall into this category. Short pasta is the easiest pasta to eat and so it's the most popular. Manufacturers, ever on the lookout to make and sell more, quickly realised that new short shapes had the most appeal and so developed this sector of the market more than any other. Ever since the 19th century competition in the pasta industry has thrived on the "design" of different short shapes, with some more successful at holding sauces than others. Among these are the frilly ballerine, fiorelli, gigli del gargano, rocchetti and spaccatella, all of which trap sauces quite well but somehow create a strange sensation in the mouth. Shapes such as banane, creste di gallo, radiatori and riccioli, are perhaps too gimmicky for their own good; so too are the mixed bags of highly colored pasta shapes, such as the seven-color orecchiette (little ears) and five-color chioccioloni (snails), which include chocolate-flavored pasta along with the more run-of-the-mill plain, tomato, squid ink and wild mushroom (porcini) varieties. These colored designer pasta shapes are often labeled *lavorazione artigianale* or *prodotto artigianale*, to indicate that they are made by artisans or local craftsmen, but they are too often disappointing, and they rarely match up to the more traditional shapes that have been tried and tested over very many years.

Five-color chioccioloni are made from plain pasta and pasta flavored with squid ink, chocolate, tomato and porcini

Spinach, plain and tomato conchiglie (hand-crafted shells designed for stuffing)

Spaccatella

Gigli del gargano

Seven-color orecchiette are made from plain pasta and pasta flavored with spinach, tomato, saffron, squid ink, beet and porcini

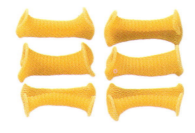

Rocchetti rigati

Fiorelli tricolori

Three-color pennoti rigati

Three-color cappelletti

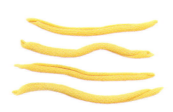

Coralli rigati

Fresh Pasta

In Italy, there has long been a tradition for buying fresh pasta, and now the custom has caught on in other countries too. Italians buy from their local *pastificio* or baker, where the beautiful window displays are such a tempting feast for the eye, while we have to content ourselves with supermarkets. Yet here too, creative talent is running wild when it comes to making fresh pasta, and the choices of different shapes, flavors and fillings are continually increasing—by popular demand. It seems that everybody loves fresh pasta, and we simply can't get enough of it. Quality is excellent, especially with the loose kinds sold in some good markets. Pre-packaged brands, although labeled fresh, are obviously not as "just-made" and silky-textured as the pasta made on a daily basis, but they are quite good nevertheless. Flavors vary, but the most common are spinach, tomato, chestnut, mushroom, beet juice, saffron, herbs, garlic, chiles and squid ink.

Buy freshly made pasta on the day you need it, or you defeat the purpose of buying it; otherwise keep it in its wrapping and use within 1–2 days of purchase (or according to the storage time given on the package). If you buy fresh pasta loose, ask the storekeeper for advice on storage. Fresh pasta is made with egg, which shortens its storage time, but on the plus side this increases its nutritional value and flavor, and gives the plain varieties a lovely sunshine-yellow color.

Fresh pasta takes much less time to cook than dried pasta, but the cooking technique is generally the same for each type. Most plain shapes will be *al dente* in 2–4 minutes, while stuffed shapes take 5–7 minutes, but always ask for advice in the store where it is made (or check the label).

The same rules apply for matching sauces to shapes as with dried pasta—long shapes are best with smooth sauces, while chunky sauces go better with short shapes.

Long and Flat Shapes

These were the first forms of fresh pasta to be available commercially, and were generally made in the local Italian markets by the proprietor or his wife. The choice used to be between plain egg tagliatelle and fettuccine, possibly flavored with spinach, but now there are many more exciting varieties. Pre-packaged long fresh pasta comes in standard shapes and sizes, but Italian markets sometimes have weekend specials when they offer different flavors and colors according to the seasonal availability of ingredients. This is often the case when a market supplies a local restaurant with fresh pasta. If a special order is made for a restaurant, the market may make extra to sell to individual customers. These occasional treats are well worth looking for, as are regional specialties. If the owners of your local Italian market are from Lazio you may find fresh homemade fettuccine on sale. Ligurians are more likely to make trenette, whereas pappardelle indicates that the owners of the shop probably have family ties with Tuscany or Bologna.

Fettuccine

These long, flat ribbon noodles are the narrow Roman version of tagliatelle, and are traditionally made about 1/4 inch wide.

They are readily available, made with egg and flavored with spinach. You may also see similar noodles called fettuccelle. The two are interchangeable, and are at their best served very simply with butter and cream.

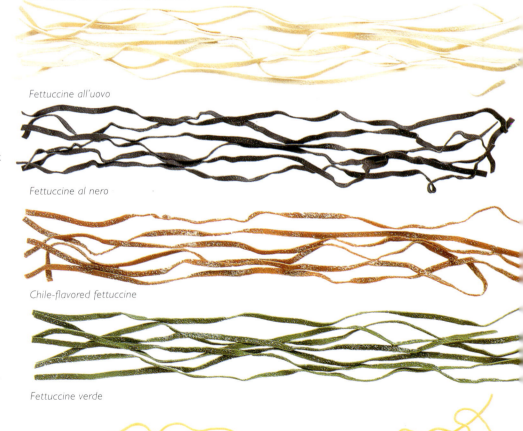

Fettuccine all'uovo

Fettuccine al nero

Chile-flavored fettuccine

Fettuccine verde

Spaghetti all'uovo

Spinach-flavored lasagne

Tomato-flavored lasagne

Lasagne all'uovo

Egg and spinach-flavored capelli d'angelo

Egg and spinach-flavored linguine

Pappardelle

Spaghetti

This pasta is widely available, in various widths. A narrow version, spaghettini, is popular, and can be found at some markets. Serve fresh spaghetti or spaghettini Neapolitan style with sauces based on olive oil and tomatoes. Both spaghetti and spaghettini are also good with fish and shellfish, as long as the pieces are cut small. Capelli d'angelo, plain or flavored with spinach, is also available.

Lasagne

Sheets of lasagne can be found plain, with egg, and flavored with spinach or tomato. Depending on the manufacturer,

they may be rectangles, squares or strips with plain or frilly edges. Lasagne al forno (baked lasagne) made with fresh sheets of pasta tastes much better than that made with dried pasta, so the fresh sheets are well worth buying.

Linguine

These look like strands of flattened spaghetti and are very narrow and thin. They are made with egg (all'uovo), and go well with a simple dressing of olive oil and flavorings, such as finely chopped garlic, chiles or freshly ground black pepper. Linguine is also good with fish and shellfish sauces.

Pappardelle

Flat egg noodles, these vary in width from 3/4–1 inch wide. Traditional pappardelle have wavy edges, but you may see them with plain edges—the main thing is that they are wider than any of the other ribbon noodles. They originated in Tuscany, but are also popular in the city of Bologna in Emilia-Romagna. In both of these regions, pasta is often served with a rich meat or game sauce, and pappardelle are the perfect choice because the noodles are wide and strong enough to support the chunkiest mixtures. Pappardelle are available plain and flavored, sometimes with sun-dried tomatoes or porcini.

Squid ink tagliolini

Tagliolini all'uovo

Salmon-flavored tagliolini

Spinach-flavored tagliolini

Tagliatelle all'uovo

Spinach-flavored tagliatelle

Tagliatelle

This is probably the best-known form of fresh pasta. The noodles are long and straight, about 1/2 inch wide. They are available everywhere, in a wide variety of flavors and colors. After plain egg tagliatelle, spinach is the most popular, but it is often flecked and flavored with fresh herbs, garlic, porcini, sun-dried tomatoes, pepper, chiles and other spices, or beautifully colored with saffron or tomato. When made with squid ink, it is black and dramatic. Tagliatelle comes from Bologna, where it is always served with Bolognese sauce, but it goes well with any meat sauce. Tagliarini and tagliolini are very thin versions of tagliatelle, about 1/8 inch wide, sold either as plain egg (*all'uovo*) or as paglia e fieno—half white and half green. Mixed packages are versatile and attractive because you can cook the different colors together or keep them separate, depending on the visual effect required. They go well with tomato and cream sauces.

SHORT SHAPES

Supermarkets and other large stores sell fresh short shapes, but the range is limited. Italian markets sometimes sell a few simple homemade shapes but because many short shapes need special machines for cutting and shaping there is seldom a wide range at small stores, and making them by hand would be too time-consuming to be commercially viable. Short shapes tend to stick together, so in supermarkets they are kept in plastic containers in the refrigerated section; these packages are useful in that they can be stored in the freezer. In some small shops excess moisture is removed by briefly fan-drying the shapes right after they are made. These are then described as semi-dried and must be sold within 24–48 hours. Shapes vary widely, depending on whether they come from large manufacturers or individual stores. Conchiglie, fusilli and penne are easy to find, while other shapes, such as garganelli and ballerine, are less widely available.

Conchiglie

These shell shapes come in different sizes and colors, and conchiglie tricolore (red, white and green) are popular. They are one of the best shapes for trapping chunky sauces. If they are ridged, so much the better. Conchiglie are also good in salads because they hold dressings well.

Fusilli

Resembling the threads of screws, these should correctly be called eliche, but they are almost always labeled fusilli. Plain, spinach and tomato flavors, either sold separately or combined, are easy to obtain. Squid ink fusilli are made in some stores. The versatile shape of this type of pasta means that it goes well with most sauces and is also good in salads.

Garganelli

Sold at some specialty markets, these are made from a very special type of egg pasta from Emilia-Romagna and look like ridged scrolls. Garganelli need to be made

Ballerine

Penne rigate

Eliche all'uovo

Conchiglie

Semi-dried garganelli

with a special tool, called *il pettine* in Italian. Squares of fresh dough are rolled around a rod and against the *pettine*, which has teeth like a comb. The teeth produce the characteristic fine ridges on the outside of the pasta. Plain and spinach flavors are available, either sold separately or combined. In Emilia-Romagna, garganelli are traditionally served with a rich meat sauce, but you can use them in any recipe that calls for short maccheroni or penne. They are especially good with rich, creamy sauces.

Penne

Sometimes called quills, these come in a variety of sizes and colors, both smooth and ribbed, just like their dried counter-part. In Rome, fresh penne is served with the chile-hot arrabbiata sauce, but it goes well with just about any sauce.

Stuffed Shapes

Until recent years, the only stuffed fresh pasta shapes available were the classic ones traditionally associated with specific regions of Italy. Ravioli was the best known shape, followed by tortellini. These regional specialties are still popular, but nowadays the traditional shapes and fillings are often varied, whether they are being made by a large-scale manufacturer or a single cook working at a local market. Individual interpretations on the basic shapes, a wide variety of fresh seasonal ingredients for the fillings, plus eye-catching color combinations for both the pasta and the fillings make variations on the theme seemingly endless. New ideas are being developed all of the time, some more successful than others, so experiment with different kinds of stuffed shapes to find the ones you like the best. Listed here are the most popular and widely available shapes, following the regional tradition.

Agnolotti

These filled pasta shapes come from northern Italy and are a specialty of Piedmont in particular. Traditionally they were shaped like plump little half moons and stuffed with meat, but this is no longer the case: nowadays you will see round and square shapes with vegetable fillings labeled as agnolotti. Square agnolotti with a pleat in the center are called *dal plin* (with a pleat). One characteristic that all agnolotti should share is a crinkled edge, made by cutting the dough around the filling with a fluted pasta wheel.

Cappelletti

These take their name from the Italian word for "little hats." In Emilia-Romagna, small squares of dough are filled and folded to make triangular shapes, then two of the ends are wrapped around and the

Semi-dried agnolotti all'uovo

Semi-dried cappelletti all'uovo

Cappelletti all'uovo stuffed with mushroom filling

Semi-dried tomato-flavored cappelletti stuffed with sun-dried tomato filling

bottom edge turned up to make a party hat shape with a brim. In some central regions of Italy, however, cappelletti are made with either plain or fluted rounds of dough instead of squares. The dough for cappelletti can be plain or egg (*all'uovo*), or flavored with tomato or spinach. Cappelletti are traditionally filled with ground meat and cheese and are eaten in northern and central regions of Italy at Christmas and New Year, especially in clear broth – *Cappelletti in brodo*. You can use them in this way or serve them as a pasta course with a little melted butter and freshly grated Parmesan cheese or, alternatively, toss the cappelletti in a tomato or cream sauce.

Fresh Pasta

Semi-dried raviolini (mini ravioli)
all'uovo with a simple ground meat filling

Oval ravioli, which are sometimes called
rotondi, stuffed with artichoke filling

Ravioli all'uovo with ground chicken filling

Handmade plain and spinach-flavored ravioli

Large rectangular ravioli stuffed with Roquefort cheese

Large ravioli stuffed with ground chicken and asparagus

Plain ravioli stuffed with asparagus filling (left), squid ink-flavored
ravioli stuffed with an herb filling and saffron-flavored ravioli
stuffed with smoked salmon and mascarpone cheese

Pansotti

Sometimes spelled pansoti, these stuffed pasta shapes are Ligurian. The word means chubby, and they are triangular in shape with little potbellies of filling in the center. It is traditional to fill pansotti with chopped cooked spinach, chopped hard-boiled eggs and grated pecorino cheese, then serve them with a walnut sauce. Pansotti are made with small squares of pasta dough and may have straight or fluted edges.

Ravioli

These are usually square with fluted edges, but size and shape vary enormously. Along with tortellini, they are the most widely made of the fresh stuffed pasta shapes, and everyone seems to have their own favorite way of making them. Plain, spinach and tomato doughs are used for the pasta (although other flavors, such as squid ink and saffron, are becoming increasingly available), and the fillings can be anything from vegetables, such as spinach, artichoke

and mushroom, to fish and shellfish, and ground veal and chicken. Very tiny ravioli are called raviolini, while the name for ravioli with a pumpkin filling is cappellacci. Tiny round ravioli are sometimes called madaglioni. Large round, oval and rectangular ravioli, stuffed with cheese or vegetable fillings, are occasionally available at Italian delicatessens and markets. Oval ravioli are sometimes called rotondi, while the large rectangular shapes may be called cannelloni rather than ravioli.

Plain and spinach-flavored tortelloni

*Sacchetti filled with a spinach and ricotta filling
and tied with thin strips of scallion*

*Tortellini stuffed with an artichoke
and truffle oil filling*

Cappelli all'uovo stuffed with minced salmon

*Tomato-flavored madaglioni all'uovo
stuffed with a shrimp and trout filling*

Sacchettini

*Candy-shaped caramelle all'uovo stuffed
with spinach and ricotta cheese*

*Spinach cannelloni stuffed with an herb
and cream cheese filling*

Tortellini

Very popular, these look more or less like
cappelletti, but are made from rounds or
circles of dough rather than squares, so
they do not have peaks. They are usually
slightly larger than cappelletti, while tortelloni and tortelli are larger still. Tortellini are
a specialty from the city of Bologna in
Emilia-Romagna, where the traditional
filling is ground meats and prosciutto
(Parma ham). At Christmas it is the local
custom to eat *Tortellini in Brodo* as a first
course soup before the main course of
roast capon or turkey. Nowadays, tortellini
are available everywhere and are eaten all
year round. There are a wide variety of
color combinations and fillings. Black squid

ink, garlic, herbs, green olive, spinach and
sun-dried tomatoes are among the many
ingredients used to flavor the dough, while
for the fillings you can choose from such
delicacies as white crab meat, pumpkin,
ricotta, asparagus, cream cheese,
caramelized onions, mushrooms,
marinated tuna, eggplant, sweet red bell
peppers, artichokes and even truffles. A
mixture of four cheeses is a popular filling.

Other stuffed pasta shapes

Creative cooks have started a trend for
making shapes that are not based on
regional traditions, so check out your local
Italian market or supermarket for the
latest shapes to arrive—you will find

new ones appearing all the time. Two very
popular pasta shapes are caramelle and
sacchetti. Caramelle means "caramel," and
this pasta shape takes its name from the
familiar shape of caramels or toffees with
their wrappings twisted at both ends. The
filling is encased in the lozenge-shaped
center and is often ricotta-cheese based,
while the pasta itself is made with egg and
may be plain, spinach-or tomato-flavored.
Sacchetti are little purses or money bags
with scrunched tops. The pasta may be
plain or flavored and the fillings based on
cheese or meat. Sacchettini are a tiny
version, most often served in soups but
also good with smooth, creamy sauces.

Equipment

Pasta demands little in the way of specialty equipment. You need to have a large saucepan for cooking the pasta and a colander for draining, while for making sauces you need only a sharp knife and a cutting board for chopping ingredients, a skillet or saucepan for cooking, and a large bowl plus spoons and forks for tossing and serving. There are a few items that will, however, make cooking and serving easier, and if you eat pasta frequently you will find them a wise investment. They are all available at good kitchenware stores and department stores.

GENERAL COOKING EQUIPMENT

You may already have some of these basic items in your kitchen.

Pasta cooking pot

Made of stainless steel, this pan has straight sides with two short handles and an inner perforated draining basket, which also has two short handles. Different sizes are available, so choose the one that suits your needs best. One that will comfortably hold at least 2½ quarts of water is adequate if you usually cook for 2–3 people, whereas a 4-quart pan is the one you will need if you often have to cook enough pasta for 6–8 servings. Pasta pots are quite expensive as pans go, but they are so practical that if you buy one you will wonder how you ever managed without it. The pasta is boiled in the inner basket, which is lifted out of the water once the pasta is *al dente*, making draining very easy and safe. This kind of pan is also quite versatile: You can use it with the draining basket for cooking or steaming vegetables or use the outer pan on its own for cooking stocks, soups, stews— and even preserves. When buying a pasta cooking pot, choose one that is not too heavy or you will find it difficult to manage once it is filled with water.

Skillet

A skillet was originally a cooking pot that stood on three or four legs in the hearth. In the United States, the term came to mean a frying pan. Nowadays, it is used on both sides of the Atlantic to describe a wide, deep pan—like a cross between a wok and a frying pan—with a long handle and a lid. This is the perfect pan for making sauces. Look for one that is at least 9 inches in diameter (10–12 inches is ideal) and 2–3 inches deep. If you often cook for a crowd or for varying numbers of people, it is worth buying two of these pans, in different sizes. Choose the best quality you can afford. Some skillets have non-stick surfaces, which is fine as long as they are of good quality.

Left: This pasta pot comes complete with an inner perforated basket for draining the pasta.

Above: A wide, deep skillet or frying pan is the ideal pan for making sauces, while a large, deep saucepan will double as a pasta pot if you don't have a specially-made one.

Left: A large, deep-bowled ladle is extremely useful. It can be used for serving broths and soups as well as for spooning sauces over pasta.

A large perforated ladle (left) and a flatter scoop (right) are ideal for lifting short pasta shapes out of boiling water.

Right: This odd-looking tool is useful for measuring spaghetti—each hole holds a different amount of pasta.

Above: These simply designed tongs can be used for lifting long strands of pasta out of boiling water.

Left: A long-handled wooden fork is the best tool to use for stirring pasta to separate the strands during cooking.

Pasta measurer

Spaghetti is difficult to put on a scale, and measuring by the handful is not always accurate. This wooden gadget has four or five holes, each of which hold enough pasta for a given number of people.

Long-handled fork

This is useful for stirring pasta during cooking to help keep the strands or pieces from sticking together. A wooden fork is better for separating pasta than a solid wooden spoon. There are also wooden pasta rakes or hooks, which look like flat wooden spoons with prongs attached to one side. They do a good job because the pasta does not slip off when it is lifted, but sometimes the teeth come unglued in the boiling water.

Tongs

Nothing is more effective for picking strands of spaghetti and long noodles out of hot water than a good pair of tongs. Sturdy stainless steel tongs are the best, preferably with long handles for safety, but the most important thing is that they feel comfortable in your hand, so check this before buying. Some tongs have awkward mechanisms, springs and hinges—the simpler the design the better. Tongs can be used for lifting out individual strands to check for doneness and for serving individual portions of long pasta.

Scoop or draining spoon

A large perforated, slotted or mesh spoon is the perfect utensil for lifting short pasta shapes out of boiling water. Choose one

that is large and deep, preferably made from stainless steel.

Ladle

For spooning sauce over pasta and for serving soups, a deep-bowled ladle is the most effective utensil. Sizes vary from small and pointed with a lip for easy pouring, to very large, functional-looking types. Stainless steel is the best material.

Parmesan knife

This is a short, quite stubby little knife with a shaped handle and blade. It is by no means an essential item, but is quite effective for scraping off shavings of Parmesan cheese from a block. It also looks good if you are serving Parmesan on a cheese board.

Below: The choice of Parmesan graters available includes a small, rotary grater with a storage space for a piece of Parmesan; a standard, stainless steel box grater; and the traditional small, hand-held Parmesan grater, which is ideal for using at the table.

Equipment for Making Pasta at Home

You can make pasta at home with nothing more sophisticated than a scale, some measuring spoons, a work surface and an ordinary rolling pin, but there are a few items of special equipment that will make the job easier. They are all available at specialty kitchenware stores and good department stores.

Tapered rolling pin

The traditional pin used in Italy for rolling out pasta dough is very long—it measures almost 32 inches in length. It is about 1 1/2 inches wide in the center and tapers almost to a point at either end. This type of rolling pin is very easy to use and is well worth buying if you enjoy making pasta by hand and don't intend to buy a special machine. A conventional, straight rolling pin can be used instead, but try to get one that is quite slim—no more than 2 inches in diameter.

Mechanical pasta machine

The same type of hand-cranked pasta machine has been used in Italian kitchens for many, many years. It has stood the test of time well, because it is still manufactured and used today, with very little modification. Made of stainless steel, it has rollers to press out the dough as thinly as possible and cutters for creating different shapes. The standard cutters usually allow you to make tagliatelle and tagliarini, but you can get attachments and accessories for other shapes,

Parmesan graters

There is a huge choice of graters, ranging from the very simple hand grater to electrically operated machines. A simple stainless steel box grater will grate Parmesan and other hard cheeses, such as pecorino, but it can be cumbersome to use with its choice of different-size teeth. It is possible to buy a small grater especially for Parmesan. This consists of a single rectangular grating plate that is designed specifically for grating hard cheese finely, and has a small handle, which can be grasped firmly. The grater is small and unobtrusive, ideal for using at the table. Mechanical Parmesan mills

are also good, as are small, hand-cranked rotary graters, and there are special Parmesan graters available, which have a box and a lid so the cheese can be stored after grating. Electric Parmesan cheese graters are only worth buying if you frequently grate a lot of cheese; a less expensive alternative is to use a small electrical chopper, the kind used for chopping herbs.

Above: The traditional Italian pasta rolling pin is very long, slightly wider in the center and narrow at both ends.

including pappardelle, ravioli and cannelloni. The machine is clamped to the edge of a work surface or table and worked by turning the handle. If you make pasta frequently, it is an excellent buy because it is inexpensive, easy and fun to use, and makes excellent pasta in a very short time. It takes all of the hard work out of making pasta by hand, and you can even get an electric motor for it so you don't have to turn the handle.

Left: The traditional hand-cranked pasta machine with rollers to press out the dough and cutters for tagliatelle and tagliarini is still one of the best ways of making pasta.

Electric Pasta Machines

Tabletop electric pasta machines mix the dough, knead it and then extrude it through cutters, so all you have to do is put the ingredients in the machine and turn it on. You can make more shapes with this type of machine than the mechanical one, but you have less control over the dough because you don't actually handle it at all. Electric pasta machines are only sold in some specialty kitchenware stores. They are expensive to buy, but are a worthwhile investment if you frequently make a lot of pasta—they can make up to $2\frac{1}{4}$ pounds at a time—and have the space to house the machine in a convenient spot.

Left: A stainless steel pasta wheel makes light work of cutting ravioli.

Pasta wheel

This is a useful gadget for cutting noodles, such as lasagne and tagliatelle, when you don't have a pasta machine, and for cutting out small stuffed shapes. The wheel can be straight or fluted, and there are some types that will cut several lengths of noodle at a time. A sharp knife can be used instead, but a pasta wheel is easier and gives a neater finish. With a pasta wheel, the pasta edges are less likely to be dragged out of shape or torn.

Above: This special metal tray is used for making mini ravioli.

sheet of dough is placed on top. The ravioli squares are cut out by rolling a rolling pin over the serrated top. This is good for making very small ravioli, which are difficult and time-consuming to make individually. Sometimes the tray is sold as a set with its own small rolling pin, or as an accessory for a pasta machine.

Ravioli cutter

This is virtually the same as a fluted cookie cutter except that it has a wooden handle and can be square or round. If you want to make square ravioli and cappelletti, you can use a pasta wheel instead of this cutter, so it isn't a vital piece of equipment. For round ravioli, tortellini and anolini you can use a round cookie cutter if you have one. The most useful sizes are 2 inches and 3 inches.

Ravioli tray

You can buy a special metal tray for making ravioli. A sheet of rolled-out dough is laid over the tray, then pressed into the indentations. The filling is then spooned into the indentations and another

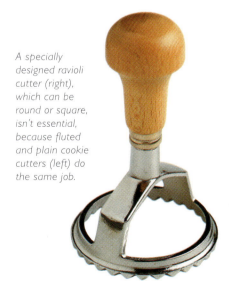

A specially designed ravioli cutter (right), which can be round or square, isn't essential, because fluted and plain cookie cutters (left) do the same job.

How to Cook and Serve Pasta

It is very easy to cook pasta properly, but without care and attention it is equally easy to cook it badly. A few simple guidelines need to be observed if pasta is to be at its best.

Once you have mastered these, you will be able to cook pasta successfully every time, no matter whether it is dried, homemade or bought fresh.

Cooking Pasta in the Microwave

Because of the large amount of water needed to boil pasta, you will not save any time by cooking it in the microwave, but for short shapes and quantities under 8 ounces, you may find it more convenient than cooking the pasta on top of the stove. The results can be quite successful. Large and long shapes, such as lasagne sheets and spaghetti, need to be cooked in batches, so there doesn't seem to be much point. Where the microwave comes into its own is in reheating pasta sauces and for reheating previously baked pasta dishes, such as lasagne and cannelloni, especially individual portions of these. The microwave is also useful for thawing and reheating sauces and baked dishes that have been stored in the freezer.

How to microwave short pasta shapes

Put the pasta in a large heatproof bowl with salt to taste and pour over boiling water to cover by 1 inch. Carefully transfer the bowl to the microwave and cook on High (100 percent power) for 3–4 minutes for fresh pasta and 8–10 minutes for dried, then let stand for 5 minutes before draining.

1 Synchronize sauce and pasta

Before starting to cook either sauce or pasta, read through the recipe carefully. It is important to know which needs to be cooked for the longest time—sometimes it is the pasta and sometimes the sauce, so don't always assume one or the other. The sauce can often be made ahead of time and reheated, and it is quite unusual for the timing of a sauce to be crucial, but pasta is almost like a hot soufflé—it waits for no one. This is especially true if you are cooking fresh pasta, for which cooking time is often only a few minutes, so the sauce needs to be ready and waiting before the pasta hits the water.

3 Use a large quantity of water

The recommended amount is 4 quarts water for every 1 pound pasta. If you are cooking less pasta than this, use at least 2½ quarts water. If there is not enough water, the pasta shapes will stick together as they swell and the pan will become over-crowded. This will result in unpleasant, gummy-textured pasta.

WATCHPOINT

It is best not to cook more than 1 1/2 pound pasta at a time, even if you have a very large saucepan, because of the danger in handling such a large amount of water. If you are using the microwave to cook pasta it is best not to cook more than 8 ounces pasta at a time. Use a large heatproof bowl, don't overfill the bowl and transfer it carefully to and from the microwave using oven mitts.

2 Use a big pan

There needs to be plenty of room for the pasta to move around in the large amount of water it requires, so a big pan is essential. The best type of pan is a tall, lightweight, straight-sided, stainless steel pasta cooking pot with its own in-built draining pan. Both outer and inner pans have two handles each, which ensure easy and safe lifting and draining. If you cook pasta a lot, it is well worth investing in one of these special pans; otherwise use the largest saucepan you have for cooking the pasta plus a large stainless steel colander, preferably one with feet for stability for draining it.

4 Get the water boiling

Before adding the pasta, the water should be at a fast rolling boil. The quickest way to do this is to boil water in the kettle, then pour it into the pasta pan, which should be set over high heat. You may need as much as 2–3 kettlefuls, so keep the water in the pan simmering, covered by the lid, while you boil the kettle again.

5 Add enough salt

Pasta cooked without salt is more or less tasteless, and with insufficient salt it is hardly any better. The recommended amount is 1 1/2–2 tablespoons salt for every 1 pound pasta. There is no need to use sea or rock salt; regular salt is perfectly acceptable. Add the salt when the water is boiling and just before you are ready to add the pasta. The water will bubble furiously just as the salt is added, which is your cue to add the pasta.

6 Add the pasta all at once

Try to get all of the pasta into the boiling water at the same time so that it will cook evenly and be ready at the same time. The quickest and easiest way is literally to shake it out of the package or the bowl of the scale, covering the surface of the water as much as possible.

7 Return the water quickly to a boil

Once the pasta is submerged in the water, give it a brisk stir with a long-handled fork or spoon and then cover the pan tightly with the lid—this will help to bring the water back to a boil as quickly as possible. Once the water is boiling, lift off the lid, turn down the heat slightly and let the water simmer over medium to high heat for the required cooking time.

8 Stir the pasta frequently during cooking

To prevent the pasta strands or shapes from sticking together, stir them frequently during cooking so they are kept constantly on the move. Use a long-handled wooden fork or spoon so you can stir right down to the bottom of the pan.

9 Drain carefully and thoroughly

If you have a pasta pot with an inner drainer, lift the draining pan up and out of the water. Shake the draining pan vigorously and stir the pasta well so that any water trapped in pasta shapes can drain out as quickly as possible. It is a good idea to reserve a few ladlefuls of the pasta cooking water in case the pasta needs a little extra moistening when it is tossed with the sauce before serving.

Accurate Timing is Essential for Cooking Pasta

Start timing the pasta from the moment the water returns to a boil after adding the pasta. Always go by the time given on the package or, in the case of fresh homemade pasta, by the time given in the recipe. For the greatest accuracy, use a kitchen timer with a bell or buzzer because even half a minute of overcooking can ruin pasta, especially if it is freshly made. Dried egg pasta is more difficult to spoil, so if you are new to pasta cooking and nervous about getting it right, start with this type.

For fresh pasta

As a general guide, thin fresh noodles will take only 2–3 minutes, thicker fresh noodles and pasta shapes 3–4 minutes, and stuffed fresh pasta 5–7 minutes.

For dried pasta

The cooking time for dried pasta will vary from 8–20 minutes depending on the type and the manufacturer. Always check the cooking time provided on the label.

Cooking Fresh Pasta

1 For freshly made pasta that has been drying on a dish towel, gather the cloth up around the pasta in a loose cylindrical shape and hold it firmly at both ends.

2 Hold the towel over the water, then let go of the end nearest to the water so that the pasta drops in.

Cooking Long Dried Pasta

1 For spaghetti you need to coil the pasta into the water as it softens. Take a handful at a time and dip it in the boiling water so that it touches the bottom of the pan.

2 As the spaghetti strands soften, coil them around using a wooden spoon or fork until they are all submerged.

Cooking Stuffed Pasta

1 Stuffed shapes require more gentle handling or they may break open and release their filling into the water, so stir them gently during cooking.

2 The best method of draining stuffed shapes after cooking is to lift them carefully out of the water with a large pasta scoop or slotted spoon (left).

When is it cooked?

The Italian term *al dente* is used to describe pasta that is cooked to perfection. Literally translated this means "to the tooth," meaning that it should be firm to the bite, which is how Italians like their pasta, and therefore how it should be served. Dried pasta, which is made from durum wheat, is always served *al dente*, whereas fresh pasta is made from a softer wheat and so is never as firm as dried, but it should still have some resistance to it. Overcooked pasta is limp and unpalatable, even slimy, and an Italian cook would not serve it. To check that the pasta is ready, test pasta frequently toward the end of the recommended cooking time by lifting out a piece with tongs, a pasta scoop or a slotted spoon and biting into it. When you are satisfied that it is done to your liking, it is time to stop the cooking.

At-a-glance Amounts

Amounts of pasta given here are intended only as a guide to the number of people they will serve. If you are cooking fresh pasta, you may need a little more than if you are using dried, but the difference is really negligible. What is more significant is whether you are serving a light or substantial sauce with the pasta.

For an Italian-style first course (primo piatto) for 4–6 people, or a main course for 2–3 people:

2½ quarts water
1 tablespoon salt
9–12 ounces fresh or dried pasta

For a first course for 6–8 people, or a main course for 4–6 people:

4 quarts water
1½–2 tablespoons salt
11 ounces–1 pound fresh or dried pasta

COOK'S TIP

If you are using an ordinary saucepan and a colander for cooking and draining pasta, have the colander ready in the sink. Carefully pour the contents of the pan into the colander, then shake the colander vigorously over the sink and stir the pasta to release any trapped water.

Combining the Pasta and Sauce

Recipes vary in the way they combine sauce and pasta. The majority have you add the sauce to the pasta, but with some it is the other way around. There are no hard-and-fast rules. If you are going to add the sauce to the drained pasta, the most important thing is to have a warmed bowl ready. The larger the bowl the better, because this will allow room for the sauce and pasta to be tossed together easily so that every piece of pasta can be thoroughly coated in sauce.

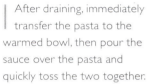

1 After draining, immediately transfer the pasta to the warmed bowl, then pour the sauce over the pasta and quickly toss the two together.

2 If the pasta is not moist enough, add a little of the pasta cooking water. Some recipes call for extra butter or oil to be added at this stage, others have grated Parmesan or pecorino cheese tossed with the pasta and sauce.

3 Use two large spoons or forks for tossing, or a large spoon and a fork. Lift the pasta and swirl it around, making sure you have scooped it up from the bottom of the bowl. The idea is to coat every piece of pasta evenly in sauce, so keep tossing until you are satisfied that this is done.

4 Occasionally, recipes call for the pasta to be returned to the cooking pan, to be combined with oil or butter and seasonings and tossed over heat until coated. A sauce may be added at this stage too, but care should be taken not to cook the pasta too much in the first place or it may overcook when it is reheated.

Serving and Presentation

Most important of all is to have your family and friends waiting at the table for the pasta, not the other way around. With the exception of baked dishes, all pasta should be eaten as soon as it is cooked and tossed with the sauce, so invite everyone to sit down just before you are ready to drain the pasta.

In most cases, pasta and sauce are tossed together in a large serving bowl in the kitchen, and the bowl is then brought straight to the table. Each person is served straight from the bowl—or the bowl is passed around the table for everyone to help themselves.

To give the pasta a finishing touch, a little Parmesan or pecorino cheese can be grated on top, or a few chopped fresh herbs, such as parsley or basil, can be sprinkled on. The choice of garnish depends on the dish and the cook, but as a general rule, grated cheese is never served with fish and shellfish sauces. For guidance, follow the garnishing instructions in individual recipes.

Occasionally, the pasta and sauce are divided among individual plates or bowls before serving—as is the practice in restaurants. This is not the traditional custom in Italian homes, but it sometimes helps to get the pasta served quickly. It is an especially good idea when you are entertaining because each individual serving can have its own attractive garnish.

Matching Sauces to Recipes

Some regional dishes are always made with the same pasta shape. *Bucatini all'Amatriciana*, *Penne all'Arrabbiata* and *Fettuccine all'Alfredo* are all classic Roman recipes, for example, and it is rare to see them served with anything other than the named pasta. The same applies to *Tagliatelle alla Bolognese* from Emilia-Romagna and *Trenette con Pesto* from Genoa. These classics are few and far between, however, and with the ever-increasing number of different shapes on the market it may seem difficult to know which sauces and shapes go well together. Happily, there are no rigid rules, and common sense usually prevails. Heavy sauces with large chunks of meat are unlikely to go well with thin spaghettini or tagliolini, simply because the chunks will slide off, so these sauces and others like them are always served with wide noodles, such as pappardelle, maccheroni and tagliatelle, or with short tubular shapes, such as penne, fusilli, conchiglie and rigatoni.

In the south of Italy, olive oil is used for cooking rather than butter, so sauces tend to be made with olive oil and they are usually served with the dried plain durum wheat pasta such as spaghetti and vermicelli that is also popular in the south. These long, thin shapes are traditionally served with tomato and seafood sauces, most of which are made with olive oil, and with light vegetable sauces. Spaghetti and vermicelli are also ideal vehicles for minimalist sauces like *Aglio e Olio* (garlic and olive oil) from Rome. Grated cheese is not normally used in these sauces, nor is it sprinkled on them.

Classic dishes, such as Bucatini all'Amatriciana (left), Penne all'Arrabbiata (below) and Fettuccine all'Alfredo (above), are almost always served with the named pasta.

Grated cheese is often tossed with pasta and sauce at the last moment, as well as being sprinkled over individual servings at the table.

In the North, butter and cream are used in sauces, and not surprisingly these go well with the egg pasta that is made there, especially fresh homemade egg pasta, which absorbs butter and cream and makes the sauce cling to it. Butter and cream also go well with tomato sauces when these are served with short shapes, especially penne, rigatoni, farfalle and fusilli.

Eating Pasta

Opinions vary as to whether pasta should be eaten from a plate or a bowl. There are no rules, so you can serve it on either. Large, shallow soup plates seem the ideal compromise, and setting each warmed soup plate on a large, cold underplate makes for easy carrying from kitchen to table.

If the recipe recommends extra Parmesan or pecorino for serving, grate the cheese just before the meal and pass it in a bowl with a small spoon so that people can help themselves. Salt and pepper shakers should also be on the table for those who like to adjust the seasoning.

Pasta is traditionally eaten with a single fork. Spaghetti and other long shapes should not be difficult to manage if they have been well tossed with the sauce. The trick is to twirl only a small amount around the fork at a time.

Wines to Serve with Pasta

It is impossible to recommend a particular wine to go with every pasta dish, but there are a few guidelines you can follow. If you know where the dish comes from, choose a wine from the same region. If a red or a white wine is used in the cooking of the sauce, select a good-quality wine for cooking and serve the rest with the meal. Otherwise, look at the main ingredient of the sauce and choose a wine that is recommended for that. Many pasta sauces are strong-tasting, garlicky or spiced with chiles, and some are served with mature Parmesan or pecorino cheese; for these you will need to choose a robust, full-flavored wine.

Barbaresco

A great red wine from Piedmont. Full-bodied and complex in flavor. Good with poultry and meat sauces.

Barbera

A medium-bodied red from Piedmont, which varies from young and slightly sparkling to rich and concentrated in flavor. Good with meat lasagne.

Bardolino

This fresh-tasting, light and fruity red from Veneto is very good to serve with poultry sauces.

Barolo

A full-bodied red made in Piedmont from Nebbiolo grapes. Good with red meat and game sauces.

Castel del Monte

Full-bodied smooth red and rosé wines from Puglia. Good with poultry and meat.

Chianti

Famous, uncomplicated red from Tuscany. Look for Chianti Classico to serve with red meat, poultry and game sauces.

Cirò

Fresh, zingy white and full-bodied red from Calabria. Drink the white with fish and shellfish sauces, the red with red meat and game sauces.

Est! Est!! Est!!!

A clean-tasting, dry white from the Lazio region. It is good with fish and shellfish sauces.

Frascati

A crisp and fruity dry white from the town of Frascati, which is near Rome in the Lazio region. Good with the very spicy Amatriciana sauce.

Lambrusco

This effervescent red from Emilia-Romagna is good with pork and rich meat sauces.

Orvieto Secco

Dry white, from the town of the same name in Umbria. Serve with fish, shellfish and poultry sauces.

Pinot Grigio

A fresh, fruity dry white from Friuli-Venezia. It is good with any sauce or pasta dish.

Soave

Light, dry white from Veneto made from Garganega grapes. It is good with any sauce or pasta dish, and is reasonably priced.

Valpolicella

Fruity red, sometimes with a bitter aftertaste, from Veneto. The name means "valley of many cellars." It is good with red meat sauces.

Valtellina

This perfumed red from Lombardy is made from Nebbiolo grapes. Look for Grumello, Inferno, Sassella and Valgella. It is good with rich meat, poultry and game sauces.

Verdicchio

Crisp, dry white with character from Marche in central Italy. It comes in a carved bottle shaped like a Roman amphora. Good with all kinds of fish and shellfish sauces.

Vernaccia

Rich, nutty red from the island of Sardinia that goes well with fish and shellfish sauces.

How to Make Pasta

Homemade pasta has a wonderfully light, almost silky texture—quite different from the so-called fresh pasta that you buy pre-packaged at some stores. If you use egg in the mixture, which is recommended if you are making pasta at home, the dough is easy to make, either by hand or machine, and the initial process is not that different from making bread. Kneading, rolling and cutting require some patience and practice, but if you invest in an inexpensive mechanical pasta machine, this part of the process will become quick and easy—and fun, too.

Pasta all'Uovo

Pasta with Eggs

The best place to make, knead and roll out pasta dough is on a wooden kitchen table, the larger the better. The surface should be warm, so marble is not suitable.

INGREDIENTS
2¾ cups flour
3 eggs
1 teaspoon salt

1 Mound the flour on a clean work surface and make a large, deep well in the center with your hands. Keep the sides of the well quite high so that when the eggs are added they will not run out of the well.

2 Crack the eggs into the well, then add the salt. With a table knife or fork, combine the eggs and salt, then gradually start incorporating the flour from the sides of the well. Try not to break the sides of the well or the runny mixture will escape and quickly spread over the work surface.

3 As soon as the egg mixture is no longer liquid, dip your fingers in the flour and use them to work the ingredients together until they form a rough and sticky dough. Scrape up any dough that sticks to the work surface with a knife, then scrape this off the knife with your fingers. If the dough is too dry, add a few drops of cold water; if it is too moist, sprinkle a little flour over it.

5 Give the dough a quarter turn counterclockwise, then continue kneading, folding and turning for 5 minutes if you intend to use a pasta machine, or for 10 minutes if you will be rolling it out by hand. The dough should be very smooth and elastic. If you are going to roll it out and cut it by hand, thorough kneading is essential.

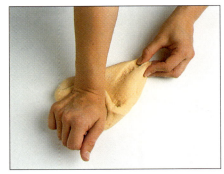

4 Press the dough into a rough ball and knead it as you would bread. Push it away from you with the heel of your hand, then fold the end of the dough back on itself so that it faces toward you and push it out again. Continue folding the dough back a little further each time and pushing it out until you have folded it back all the way toward you and all the dough has been kneaded.

6 Wrap the dough in plastic wrap and let it rest for 15–20 minutes at room temperature. It will then be ready to roll out.

COOK'S TIP

Don't skimp on the kneading time or the finished pasta will not be light and silky.

If you have a food processor, you can save a little time and effort by using it for making pasta dough. It will not knead the dough adequately, however, so you may find it just as quick and easy to make it by hand, especially if you take into account the washing and drying of the bowl and blade. The ingredients are the same as when making pasta by hand.

1 Put the flour and salt in the bowl of a food processor fitted with the metal blade.

2 Add 1 whole egg and then pulse-blend until the ingredients are mixed.

3 Turn the food processor on at full speed and add the remaining whole eggs through the feeder tube. Keep the machine running for just long enough to let dough to be formed.

4 Turn the dough out onto a clean work surface. Knead as when making pasta by hand, then wrap in plastic wrap and let rest at room temperature for 15–20 minutes.

Making Pasta Shapes by Hand

Once you have made your pasta dough and let it rest, it is ready to be rolled out and cut into various shapes. If you don't have a pasta machine, the following steps show how to do it by hand. The technique is quite hard work, and the pasta may not be quite as thin as that made in a machine, but it is equally good nevertheless. If you enjoy making your own pasta and think you would like to make it regularly, it is well worth buying a mechanical pasta machine to save you both time and effort.

1 Unwrap the ball of dough and cut it in half. Roll and cut one half at a time, keeping the other half wrapped in plastic wrap as before.

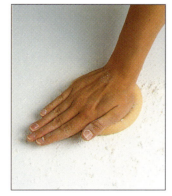

2 Sprinkle a very large, clean work surface lightly with flour. Put the unwrapped dough on the surface, sprinkle it with a little flour and flatten it with the heel of your hand. Turn the dough over and repeat the process to form the dough into a 5-inch disk.

3 Using a lightly floured rolling pin, start to roll the dough out. Always roll the dough away from you, stretching it outward from the center and moving the dough around a quarter turn after each rolling. If the dough gets sticky, sprinkle the rolling pin, dough and work surface lightly with flour.

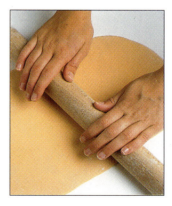

4 Continue rolling, turning and stretching the dough until it is a large oval, as thin as you can possibly get it. Ideally it should be about 1/8-inch thick. Try to get it even all over or the shapes will not cook in the same length of time. Don't worry if the edges are not neat; this is not important.

Cutting Ribbon Noodles

1 Before you begin, have ready plenty of clean dish towels lightly dusted with flour; you will need to spread the shapes out on them after cutting. Dust the sheet of pasta (called *la sfoglia* in Italian) lightly with flour. Starting from one long edge, roll up the sheet into a loose cylinder.

2 With a large sharp knife, cut cleanly across the pasta roll. Cut at ½-inch intervals for tagliatelle, slightly narrower (about ¼-inch) for fettuccine, and as narrow as you can possibly get for tagliarini or capelli d'angelo. Take care not to drag the knife, or the edges of the ribbons will be ragged.

3 With floured fingers, unravel the rolls on the work surface, then toss the noodles lightly together on the floured dish towels, sprinkling them with more flour.

4 Repeat the rolling and cutting with the remaining pasta. Let the strips dry on the dish towels for at least 15 minutes before cooking, tossing them occasionally and sprinkling them with a little flour if they become sticky.

Cutting Pappardelle

1 Using a fluted pasta wheel, cut the pasta sheet into long strips about ¾–1 inch wide. Try to keep the strips the same width or they will not cook evenly.

2 Spread the pappardelle strips out in a single layer on floured dish towels and sprinkle them with a little more flour. Let the pappardelle dry on the towels for at least 15 minutes before cooking.

Cutting Lasagne and Cannelloni

1 With a large sharp knife, cut the pasta sheets into 5–6 x 3–4-inch rectangles or whatever size fits your baking dish best.

2 Spread the rectangles out in a single layer on floured dish towels, sprinkle them with more flour and let dry for at least 15 minutes before cooking. They can be used for both lasagne and cannelloni.

COOK'S TIP

Don't throw away the trimmings when making pasta shapes, such as tagliatelle and lasagne—cut the trimmings into small pieces and pop them into soup at the last minute. You can cut leftover scraps into any rough shape you like, but there are two shapes that are made especially for soups: quadrucci and maltagliati.

Cutting Quadrucci (for Soups)

1 Stack two pasta sheets on top of each other, with a light sprinkling of flour in between. With a large sharp knife, cut the pasta diagonally into 1½-inch wide strips, then cut across the strips in the opposite direction to make 1½-inch squares.

2 Spread the squares out on floured dish towels and sprinkle with more flour. Let dry for at least 15 minutes before cooking.

Cutting Maltagliati (for Soups)

1 Dust one pasta sheet lightly with flour. Starting from one long edge, roll the sheet up into a cylinder. Lightly flatten the cylinder, then, with a sharp knife, slice off the corners at one end, making two diagonal cuts to form two sides of a triangle. Cut straight across to complete the triangle. Repeat all the way along the cylinder, then unfold the maltagliati.

2 Spread out the maltagliati on floured dish towels. Sprinkle the shapes with a little more flour and let them dry for at least 15 minutes before cooking.

COOK'S TIP

Maltagliati means badly cut, so don't worry if the pasta is misshapen—it is meant to be. Quadrucci and maltagliati can also be cut from fresh lasagne rectangles, but this will take slightly longer.

Making Short Pasta Shapes

Most small pasta shapes are best left to the professionals, because they either take too long to make or require specialty equipment. There are a couple of shapes that are an exception: garganelli and

farfalle. Garganelli are traditionally made with a special tool called *il pettine*, but you can improvise with an old-fashioned butter paddle and a round pencil.

Making Garganelli

1 Cut the pasta sheets into 2-inch squares. Lay the butter paddle ridges horizontally on the work surface, with the ridges facing toward you. Angle the square so that it is diamond-shaped and place it over the ridges. Put a pencil diagonally across the corner of the square that is closest to you.

2 Roll the pasta square up around the pencil, pressing down hard on the ends of the pencil as you go. The ridges of the butter paddle will imprint themselves on the pasta.

3 Stand the pencil upright on the work surface and tap the end so that the tube of pasta slides off.

4 Spread the garganelli out in a single layer on floured dish towels, sprinkle them with more flour and let them dry for at least 15 minutes before cooking.

Making Farfalle

1 With a fluted pasta wheel, cut the pasta sheets into rectangles measuring 1¼ x 1-inch. Pinch the long sides of each rectangle between your index finger and thumb and squeeze hard to make a bow-tie shape. If the pasta will not hold the shape, moisten your fingers with water and squeeze again.

2 Spread the farfalle out in a single layer on floured dish towels, sprinkle them with a little more flour and let dry for at least 15 minutes before cooking.

Making Pasta Shapes Using a Machine

Rolling the Dough

A machine makes light work of rolling pasta dough. It makes thinner, smoother pasta than you can make by hand, and the thickness is always even. Some shapes, such as lasagne, are cut by hand, but for cutting noodles, a machine is invaluable.

1 Clamp the machine securely to your work surface and insert the handle in the roller slot. Set the rollers at their widest setting and sprinkle them lightly with flour. Unwrap the ball of pasta and cut it into quarters. Work with one quarter at a time, wrapping the other three pieces of pasta dough in plastic wrap.

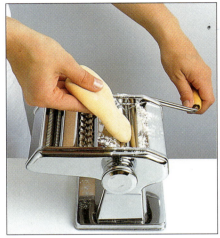

2 Flatten the quarter of dough with lightly floured hands and make it into a rough rectangle, just a little narrower in width than the rollers of the machine. Feed this through the rollers of the machine.

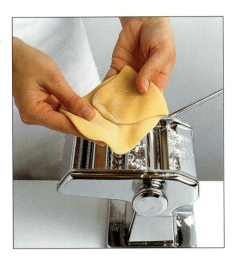

3 Fold the dough into thirds, then feed it lengthwise through the rollers. Repeat the folding and rolling five times.

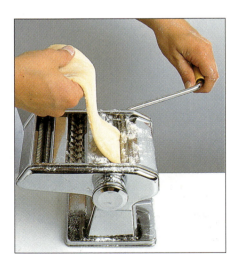

4 Turn the roller setting one notch. Sprinkle the pasta lightly with flour and feed it through the rollers again, only this time unfolded.

5 Turn the roller setting another notch and repeat the rolling, then continue in this way without folding the dough until you get to the last setting, turning the roller setting another notch after each rolling and sprinkling it lightly with flour if it becomes sticky. The dough will get longer and thinner with every rolling until it reaches 35 inches–3 feet in length. Once the dough has been rolled, it is ready for cutting into the required shape.

COOK'S TIPS

•About halfway through the rolling process, you may find that the pasta strip becomes too unwieldy and difficult to handle because it is so long. In this case, cut the strip in half or into thirds and work with one piece at a time. Remember to return the notch on the roller to the setting where you left off when you start with the next piece of dough.

•You may find that the dough is thin enough on the penultimate setting, in which case you can stop there. This will definitely be the case if you are going to make tonnarelli or spaghetti alla chitarra.

•Keep sprinkling the pasta dough lightly with flour if it becomes sticky, and keep the rollers lightly floured to prevent the pasta from sticking to the machine.

•Any trimmings and leftover pieces of pasta dough can be re-rolled and more shapes can be cut from them.

•Once they are dry, noodles and pasta shapes can be stored in a paper bag for 3–4 days, or frozen in plastic bags for up to 1 month.

Cutting Lasagne and Cannelloni

1 Using a sharp knife, cut the rolled pasta strip into 5–6 x 3–4-inch rectangles, or whatever size fits your baking dish best.

2 Spread out the rectangles in a single layer on floured dish towels and sprinkle with flour.

COOK'S TIPS

•Let the lasagne sheets dry on the dish towels while rolling and cutting the remaining three pieces of dough.
•Stack each successive batch of lasagne sheets on top of the previous one, with a floured dish towel in between.

Cutting Tagliatelle and Fettuccine

1 Insert the handle in the slot for the widest cutters and sprinkle these cutters lightly with flour. Cut the pasta strip to about 12 inches long if you haven't done so already, and sprinkle it lightly with flour. Feed the pasta through the widest cutters.

2 Continue turning the handle of the pasta machine slowly and steadily, guiding the strands with your other hand.

3 Toss the tagliatelle or fettuccine in flour and spread the noodles out on a floured dish towel. Let dry while rolling and cutting the remaining dough.

Cutting Tonnarelli and Spaghetti alla Chitarra

1 Stop rolling the pasta strip after the second to last or next to last setting, then insert the handle in the slot for the narrowest cutters and feed the pasta through the machine.

2 Proceed as for tagliatelle or fettuccine, turning the handle and guiding the long strands with your other hand. Toss the tonnarelli or spaghetti in flour and spread out on floured dish towels.

COOK'S TIP

When making spaghetti alla chitarra, the thickness and width of the pasta should be equal so the noodles come out square. You may need to experiment with this shape a few times until you get it just the right thickness.

VARIATIONS

To make tagliarini or spaghettini, insert the pasta machine handle in the slot for the narrowest cutters and proceed as for tonnarelli and spaghetti alla chitarra.

Making Ravioli

1 Using a large sharp knife, cut the rolled pasta strip into two 18–20-inch lengths, if this has not been done already.

2 Using a teaspoon, put 10–12 little mounds of your chosen filling along one side of one of the pasta strips, spacing them evenly.

3 Using a pastry brush, carefully brush a little water onto the pasta strip around each mound of filling.

4 Fold the plain side of the pasta strip over the filling.

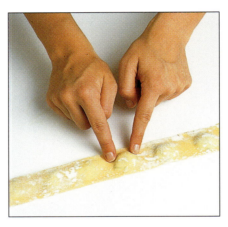

5 Starting from the folded edge, press down gently with your fingertips around each mound, pushing the air out at the unfolded edge. Sprinkle lightly with flour.

6 With a fluted pasta wheel, cut along each long side, then in between each mound to make small square shapes.

7 Put the ravioli on floured dish towels, sprinkle lightly with more flour and let dry while repeating the process with the remaining dough. For a 3-egg dough, you should get 80–96 ravioli, more if you re-roll the trimmings.

COOK'S TIPS

•*Ravioli made in this way are not perfectly square, but they look charmingly homemade. If you prefer a more precise finish, you should use a ravioli tray, which you can buy at specialty kitchenware store. The ravioli tray can be bought on its own or as an extra accessory to a pasta machine. Another alternative is to use a hand-held ravioli cutter or a round plain or fluted cookie cutter.*
•*Have ready 3 or 4 floured dish towels before you begin cutting the pasta shapes. Arrange the stuffed shapes on the towels, well-spaced and in one layer, because if you overlap them, they may stick together.*
•*Once they are dry, stuffed pasta shapes can be frozen for up to 1 month, layered between sheets of plastic wrap in plastic bags.*

Fillings for Stuffed Pasta
These vary from one or two simple ingredients to special traditional recipes. The ingredients are combined and often bound with beaten egg. Seasoning is added to taste.

Simple ideas
•*spinach, Parmesan, ricotta and nutmeg*
•*crab, mascarpone, lemon, parsley and chiles*
•*taleggio cheese and fresh marjoram*

Regional specialities
•*ground pork and turkey with fresh herbs, ricotta and Parmesan*
•*fresh herbs, ricotta, Parmesan and garlic*
•*puréed cooked pumpkin, prosciutto, mozzarella and parsley*

Making Agnolotti

1 Using a sharp knife, cut the rolled strip of pasta dough by hand into two 18–20-inch lengths, if this has not been done already.

2 Using a teaspoon, put 8–10 little mounds of your chosen filling along one side of one of the pasta strips, spacing them evenly.

3 Using a pastry brush, carefully brush a little water onto the pasta strip around each mound of filling.

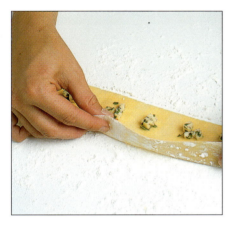

4 Fold the plain side of the pasta strip over the filling.

5 Starting from the folded edge, press down gently with your fingertips around each mound, pushing the air out at the unfolded edge. Sprinkle lightly with flour.

6 Using only half of a 2-inch fluted round ravioli or cookie cutter, cut around each mound of filling to make a half-moon shape.

7 If desired, press the cut edges of the agnolotti with the tines of a fork to give a decorative effect.

8 Put the agnolotti on floured dish towels, sprinkle lightly with more flour and let dry while repeating the process with the remaining dough. For a 3-egg dough, you should get 64–80 agnolotti, more if you re-roll the trimmings.

COOK'S TIPS

•When cutting out the agnolotti, make sure that the folded edge is the straight edge.
•Don't re-roll the trimmings after cutting each pasta strip, but wait until you have done them all. If there is no filling left for the rolled pasta trimmings, you can use them to make noodles or small shapes for soup.

Making Tortellini / Tortelloni

1 Using a sharp knife, cut the rolled strip of pasta dough by hand into two 18–20-inch lengths, if this has not been done already.

2 To make tortellini: with 2-inch fluted ravioli or cookie cutter, cut out 8–10 disks from one of the pasta strips. For tortelloni use a 2¹/₂-inch cutter.

3 Using a teaspoon and a fingertip, put a little mound of your chosen filling in the center of each disk.

4 Brush a little water around the edge of each disk.

5 Fold the disk in half over the filling so that the top and bottom edges do not quite meet. Press to seal.

6 Wrap the half-moon shape around an index finger and pinch the ends together to seal.

7 Put the tortellini or tortelloni on floured dish towels, sprinkle with flour and let dry while repeating the process with the remaining dough. For a 3-egg dough, you should get 64–80 tortellini, more if you re-roll the trimmings.

Making Pansotti and Cappelletti / Cappellacci

Pansotti are made from 2-inch squares of pasta that are folded in half over the filling to make triangles. Moisten the edges of the triangles and press to seal in the filling.

Cappelletti and cappellacci are made in the same way as tortellini, using squares of pasta rather than disks. The edges are turned up so they look like little hats.

Making Flavored and Colored Pasta

There are many different ingredients you can use to change the flavor and color of pasta, whether you are making the dough by hand or machine, although you will find it easier to get a more even color with a machine. Some flavors are more trouble than they are worth, so it is best to restrict your choice to the tried and tested ones. The following flavorings are the most successful, and the amounts of ingredients given are for a 3-egg batch of *pasta all'uovo* (pasta dough with eggs).

Black pepper

Chile

Porcini

Tomato

Black pepper

Put 2 tablespoons black peppercorns or mixed peppercorns in a mortar and crush them coarsely with a pestle. Add to the eggs in the well before you start to incorporate the flour.

Chile

Add 1–2 teaspoons crushed dried red chiles to the eggs in the well before you start to incorporate the flour.

Porcini

Soak 1/2 ounce porcini (dried wild mushrooms) in 3/4 cup warm water. Drain the porcini and squeeze to remove as much water as possible. Dry the mushrooms thoroughly on paper towels, then chop them finely and add them to the eggs in the well before you start to incorporate the flour. The dough will be stickier than usual, so you will need to add more flour during kneading, rolling and cutting. If desired, you can add the porcini soaking water to the water for boiling the pasta. This will intensify the mushroom flavor of the pasta.

Tomato

Add 2 tablespoons tomato paste to the eggs in the well before you start to incorporate the flour. The pasta dough will be stickier than usual, so you will need to add more flour during kneading, rolling and cutting.

Spinach

Wash 5 ounces fresh spinach leaves and place them in a large saucepan with only the water that clings to the leaves. Add a pinch of salt, then cover the pan and cook over medium heat for about 8 minutes or until the spinach is wilted and tender. Drain the spinach, let sit for a few minutes until cool enough to handle, then squeeze it hard in your hands to remove as much water as possible. Dry the spinach thoroughly on several sheets of paper towel, then finely chop it using a large sharp knife or a food processor and add it to the eggs in the well before you start to incorporate the flour. The pasta dough will be much stickier than usual, so you will need to add a little extra flour during kneading and when rolling and cutting the dough.

Squid ink

Add 8 grams of squid ink to the eggs in the well before you start to incorporate the flour. The dough will be stickier than usual, so you will need to add more flour during kneading, rolling and cutting.

Herb

Wash and dry three small handfuls of fresh herbs. Basil, flat leaf parsley, sage and thyme are all good choices, either singly or together. Finely chop the herbs and add them to the eggs in the well before you start to incorporate the flour. The dough may be a little more sticky than usual, in which case you may need to add a little extra flour during kneading and when rolling and cutting it.

Saffron

Sift 3 or 4 sachets of saffron powder with the flour before starting to make the pasta dough.

Spinach

Squid ink

Herb

Saffron

Making Striped Pasta

You can use different colors to make striped dough that can be cut into rectangles for lasagne and cannelloni. It is quite tricky, and the rolling out is best done with a pasta machine.

Plain or saffron yellow and spinach doughs look very good together, and another excellent combination is plain or saffron yellow dough contrasted with dough colored with tomato or squid ink. To make pasta tricolore (three-colored pasta), mix stripes of tomato dough, squid ink or spinach dough and plain dough. Some creative chefs make checked and plaid patterns with colored pasta, but this is very time-consuming for the home cook.

1 Roll out two different colored pieces of dough on a pasta machine, keeping them separate and taking them up to and including the second to last setting.

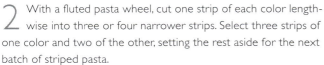

2 With a fluted pasta wheel, cut one strip of each color lengthwise into three or four narrower strips. Select three strips of one color and two of the other, setting the rest aside for the next batch of striped pasta.

3 The aim is to join the pasta strips together, using water as glue. Brush one long edge of one pasta strip with a little water, then join a pasta of a different color to it, placing it over the moistened edge and pressing it firmly to seal the join. Repeat this process, alternating the pasta colors until you have a length of pasta that resembles a scarf, with three stripes of one color and two stripes of the other.

4 Sprinkle the pasta liberally with flour, lift it very carefully and put it through the pasta machine, which should be set to the next to last setting.

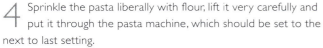

5 Cut the dough into rectangles or squares for cannelloni or lasagne and spread these out in a single layer on floured dish towels. Sprinkle them with flour and let dry for at least 15 minutes before cooking.

COOK'S TIPS

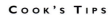

• When cutting flavored tagliatelle or tagliarini on a pasta machine, sprinkle the cutters liberally with flour before putting the dough through. The noodles tend to stick together as they come through the machine, so you may need to separate them gently with floured hands before putting them on dish towels and tossing them in more flour.

• When cooking flavored pasta, start testing for doneness earlier than usual. The ingredients added for some flavors make the pasta more moist and soft than usual, and this means that it cooks a little more quickly.

• You can use striped pasta for making ravioli: keep the strips fairly narrow and make sure they are well sealed, otherwise the ravioli may split open during cooking.

Making Silhouette Pasta

Fresh herbs can be rolled between sheets of pasta for a very pretty decorative effect. The pasta needs to be very thin, so it is best to roll it out on a pasta machine. Use only soft, leafy herbs, such as flat-leaf parsley, chervil, green or purple basil or sage. Silhouette pasta can be boiled and served with melted butter and grated Parmesan, or cooked in a clear soup (*in brodo*).

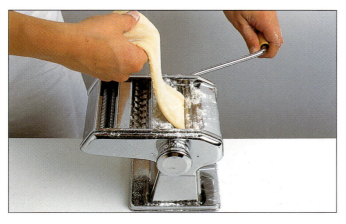

1 Roll out a piece of dough on a pasta machine, taking it up to and including the last setting. Moisten one side of the strip of dough lightly with water. A mister or spray bottle is ideal for this.

Above: Fresh herbs, such as basil (top left), flat-leaf parsley (left) and sage (right), can be rolled between sheets of dough to make pretty silhouette pasta.

2 Arrange individual fresh herb leaves on the moistened half of the dough, placing them at regular intervals. Fold the dry half of the dough over the herbs and press the edges firmly to seal.

3 Sprinkle the pasta liberally with flour and put it through the machine, on the penultimate setting.

4 With a floured pasta wheel, cut around each herb leaf to make square ravioli shapes. Spread the shapes out in a single layer on floured dish towels. Sprinkle them with more flour and let dry for at least 15 minutes before cooking.

As an alternative to using a pasta wheel for cutting out rectangular shapes, use a small, fluted cookie cutter and stamp out round shapes.

The Pasta Pantry

Certain ingredients crop up time and time again in sauces for pasta. Some can be kept in the pantry, while fresh ones must either be bought just before use, or kept in the refrigerator. Fresh herbs and leaves, spices, oils, vinegars and other less well-known ingredients are used to add flavor. Canned and dried fish and shellfish are useful additions to your pantry, while fresh vegetables, such as eggplant, tomatoes and bell peppers, along with garlic and sun-dried vegetables, play an important part in many pasta dishes. Cheese and cream are used in sauces, in fillings and for baked pasta dishes.

FRESH HERBS AND LEAVES

These are used extensively for flavoring sauces for pasta, and for presentation and garnishing. Italian cooks keep pots of fresh herbs growing on the windowsill or in the garden, and think nothing of tossing in a handful of this or that herb to freshen up the flavor of their cooking. Herbs are added according to the individual cook's taste, and are seldom measured.

Basil

Basil
Basilico

The variety known as sweet basil is used in Italian cooking, and this is the one you are most likely to find in stores. It is used all over Italy, but most of all in Liguria, where it grows prolifically and is used in large quantities for pesto. Basil has a special affinity with tomatoes and is frequently used with them in sauces for pasta. It is best torn or shredded and added at the last moment. Fine chopping and long cooking spoil its pungent flavor.

Bay
Alloro/lauro

Both fresh and dried bay leaves are used all over Italy for flavoring soups and broths and long-cooking sauces, especially those made with meat, poultry and game. The leaves are removed before serving.

Bay leaves

Marjoram

Marjoram and Oregano
Maggiorana e Origano

These two herbs are closely related, but their flavors are quite different. Marjoram is sweet and delicate, while oregano, a wild variety of marjoram, is a pungent herb that should be used sparingly. They are both used in sauces for pasta, especially tomato-based ones, but marjoram is used more in Liguria and the north of Italy and oregano in the south, where it is perhaps best known for being sprinkled on pizza. Both marjoram and oregano are best chopped quite finely. They are sometimes used dried in the winter.

Oregano

Mint
Mentuccia

Mint is not an herb usually associated with Italian cooking, but it is frequently used in Roman dishes, in the cooking of central Italy, and even as far south as Calabria. Mentuccia is a particular kind of wild mint with small leaves grown in Rome, and there is also another variety called nepitella. You may come across the flavor of fresh mint in pasta soups, and very occasionally in sauces for pasta.

Mint

Parsley
Prezzemolo

Italians use the flat-leaf variety of parsley, which is also sold as Italian parsley. It looks very similar to cilantro, and has a stronger flavor than curly parsley. It is used frequently in sauces for pasta, in fairly large amounts, and is often roughly chopped and fried in olive oil with a *battuto* of onion and garlic at the beginning of sauce making. It is popular all over Italy and is only used fresh.

Flat leaf parsley

Radicchio

Radicchio di Treviso

Radicchio di Verona

Arugula

Arugula
Rucola

Peppery *rucola* loses its pungency when cooked, so it is added to pasta sauces at the last minute, or strewn liberally on top of pasta dishes just before serving. Bunches of large-leaved *rucola* from the greengrocer are best; the small packets sold at supermarkets are very expensive and seem to lack flavor. Use *rucola* as soon as possible after purchase because the leaves can quickly go limp and yellow, especially in warm weather.

Radicchio

This ruby red and white salad leaf is a member of the chicory family. The most common variety, *radicchio di Verona*, is small and round with very tightly furled leaves, but there is another type called *radicchio di Treviso*, which is streaked creamy white and red with looser, long and tapering leaves. Both have a bitter flavor, which is much appreciated in small amounts in pasta sauces. Shredded leaves should be added at the last moment, to preserve their color.

Rosemary

Rosemary
Rosmarino

This most fragrant and pungent herb is very popular all over Italy. Rosemary is used sparingly in meat and tomato sauces, either very finely chopped or on the sprig, which is then removed from the sauce before serving. Dried rosemary is sometimes used in the winter months.

Sage
Salvia

Along with parsley, basil and rosemary, sage is one of Italy's favorite herbs. It is frequently used by Roman cooks who sizzle fresh sage in butter to create a classic sauce to serve with ravioli. Fresh sage leaves are also used with meat, sausage, poultry and game sauces, either finely shredded or chopped or as whole leaves, which are removed before serving. Fresh sage is preferred to dried, but dried sage is occasionally used in the winter, in sauces that are cooked for a long time.

Sage

Thyme
Timo

This aromatic and distinctively flavored herb is used both fresh and dried. It is a Mediterranean herb that goes well with tomato-based sauces and with meat and poultry, and it is also good mixed with rosemary and bay.

Thyme

SPICES AND SALT

Spicy, highly seasoned foods are not normally associated with Italian cooking, but the use of spices in cooking dates back to Roman—and even Etruscan—times, when spices were used freely, often to excess. Nowadays, spices tend to be used more sparingly and the range tends to be limited to a few favorites.

Dried chiles

Fresh chiles

Chile flakes

Chile
Peperoncino

Small red chiles are immensely popular in the south of Italy and Sardinia, and they are frequently used in sauces for pasta. Sometimes the sauce is a classic that depends on chiles for its essential flavor— the hot and spicy *Penne all'Arrabbiata* from Rome being perhaps the most famous. Most often, however, chiles are added more sparingly with the aim of livening up a sauce and intensifying its flavor rather than giving it a fiery punch.

Fresh chiles tend to be fried with a *soffritto* of olive oil, onion, garlic and parsley at the beginning of sauce making, whereas dried chiles are popped into the sauce when it is bubbling. Both fresh and dried chiles are often added whole to sauces in order to impart a subtle flavor. They are later lifted out and either discarded or chopped or crumbled, then returned to the sauce. The seeds may be included or left out, depending on the degree of heat required (the seeds contain most of the heat). Crushed dried red chiles or chile flakes (sold in little jars) are very handy when just a pinch or two of chile is required in a recipe.

Cinnamon
Cannella

Ground cinnamon is used in stuffings for pasta, both with meat and cheese. It gives a fragrant aroma and subtle sweetness and is always used sparingly.

Nutmeg
Noce moscata

Whole nutmeg is grated fresh when needed. It is used for flavoring *la beschiamella* (béchamel sauce) and is often used in combination with spinach and ricotta cheese. In Emilia-Romagna, it is traditionally used for flavoring meat sauces and stuffings for pasta.

Pepper
Pepe

Black peppercorns are ground fresh from a pepper mill as and when they are needed, both in cooking and at the table. Black pepper is used in just about every pasta sauce that is made, and it is also used to speckle and flavor homemade pasta. If coarsely crushed peppercorns are required, they are ground with a mortar and pestle.

Saffron
Zafferano

The most expensive spice in the world, saffron comes in two different forms. Threads of saffron, the actual dried stigmas of the crocus, are usually wrapped in cellophane and sold in sachets. They can be sprinkled into a sauce, but are more often soaked in warm water for 20–30 minutes, so that the water can be strained off and used for coloring and flavoring. Saffron powder is sold in sachets and can be sprinkled directly into sauces. It is less

Saffron

expensive than the threads and considered by many to be inferior, but it is more convenient to use. Saffron has a delicate but distinctive flavor, which is good with both cream and butter-based sauces as well as fish and shellfish. The spice is also used to color homemade pasta.

Salt
Sale

Coarse sea salt and rock salt are ground in a salt mill and used both as a seasoning in cooking and at the table. It is essential that salt is added to the water when boiling pasta to give it flavor, but for this you can use refined cooking salt rather than the more expensive sea or rock salt. Just about every pasta sauce will have salt as a seasoning, except perhaps those containing salty anchovies or bottarga (air-dried mullet or tuna roe).

Peppercorns (left) and sea salt

OILS AND VINEGARS

Oil and vinegar are essential pantry items for the Italian cook. Don't buy cheap brands; it's not worth it. Good olive oil and wine or balsamic vinegar will lift the flavor of a sauce or salad and enhance the other ingredients in it.

Olive oil
Olio d'oliva

Extra virgin olive oil is the best and most expensive of the olive oils. This is the oil that is secreted when the olives are crushed mechanically by cold presses.

No other processing or any heat is involved in the making of extra virgin olive oil. It should have an acidity level of one percent or less, but as this information is seldom on the label of the bottle, this is difficult to check.

Extra virgin is the oil to use for salads, since heating may spoil its natural olive flavor. It is also the one to use for sprinkling on warm food or for tossing with pasta in dishes, such as *Spaghetti Aglio e Olio*, that rely on olive oil for their predominant flavor.

Fruity, often peppery, Tuscan oil is reputed to be among the best of the extra virgin olive oils, although some cooks prefer oil from Umbria, or from Veneto or Liguria, which are more delicate. Oils from the South are stronger and more intensely flavored, and these may be more to your taste. Brands vary enormously, so experiment to find what suits you best.

For cooking and heating, virgin olive oil is the one to use. This is less expensive than extra virgin because it has a higher acidity

Virgin olive oil (left), extra virgin olive oil (center) and balsamic vinegar (right)

level (up to four percent), but it is cold pressed and not refined in any way so it still has a good, full flavor. Many pasta sauces start with the frying of flavoring ingredients, such as onion, garlic, celery, parsley, chiles and carrot. If these are fried in an oil with a good flavor, the sauce will have a strong base (*soffritto*), the flavor of which will then permeate through the other ingredients during cooking.

Vinegar
Aceto

Occasionally a splash of red or white wine vinegar may be added to a pasta sauce, but wine vinegar is more often used in salad dressings. Flavorwise, red and white vinegars are interchangeable, but the color of the salad ingredients may dictate whether you use red or white.

Balsamic vinegar (aceto balsamico) from Modena in Emilia-Romagna is a different thing altogether. It is a dark, syrupy vinegar that is aged in wooden casks for many years. The best and most authentic *aceto balsamico* will have been aged in casks or barrels of different woods for 40–50 years. Labeled *tradizionale di Modena*, this vinegar is only used a drop at a time, usually at the moment of serving, on fish or meat, salads and even fresh strawberries. For flavoring a pasta sauce or salad, use the much less expensive balsamic vinegar that has been aged between five and ten

years. Its flavor does not compare with the genuine article, but it is musky and slightly sweet, and very good.

FLAVORINGS

Some special ingredients are used in different regions of Italy, and you may need to buy them for a particular sauce.

Salted capers

Capers bottled in brine

Capers
Capperi

Capers are the fruit of a flowering shrub that grows in the Mediterranean. They are sold in various ways. The best are the large, salted capers sold in small jars at Italian markets. Check before buying that the salt is white and has not discolored at all. Yellow salt is a sign that the capers are past their best and may have a rancid taste. Before use, salted capers need to be soaked in several changes of water for 10–15 minutes, then drained, rinsed in fresh water and dried, but after this initial preparation they taste very fresh and good. They can be chopped and used to add piquancy to sauces—you will often find them in recipes from the south of Italy and Sicily and Sardinia.

It is also possible to buy tiny capers sold in small bottles of brine or vinegar. These have a strong flavor and should be rinsed well before use. Despite this, they almost always taste sharp and vinegary, so chop them very finely and use them sparingly.

Olives
Olive

Both black and green olives are used in making sauces and salads, although black olives are more highly favored. The best type for pasta sauces are the small, shiny, very black *gaeta* olives from Liguria. Buy the plain ones for cooking, not those with additional flavorings, such as herbs, garlic, chiles and other spices, which are intended for antipasto. Olives are best added to a sauce toward the end of cooking. They need no cooking, only heating through, and if added too early they can impart a bitter flavor. When using olives in a pasta sauce or salad, pit them first, because the pits are awkward to manage when you are eating pasta.

Olives

Pancetta
Pancetta

This is cured belly of pork, the Italian equivalent of bacon, which has a spicy, sweet flavor and aroma. Unsmoked pancetta is sold in a roll at Italian deli-catessens, and is called pancetta arrotolata or pancetta coppata. A machine is used to slice it very thinly to order and it can be eaten as it is for an antipasto, or cut into strips or diced for use in cooking. Pancetta affumicata is smoked and comes in strips, which look like bacon complete

Smoked (left) and unsmoked pancetta

with rind. There is a version called pancetta stesa, which is long and flat. Smoked pancetta is cut into strips or dice and used as the base for ragù and many other pasta sauces, the most famous of which is carbonara. Some supermarkets sell packages of diced pancetta. The quality and flavor are generally good, so these are well worth buying for convenience. If you are unable to get pancetta, bacon can be used instead, and you can buy smoked or unsmoked, whichever flavor you prefer.

Pine nuts
Pinoli

Best known for their inclusion in pesto, these small, creamy white nuts have an unusual waxy texture and resinous flavor. They look and taste good sprinkled on pasta salads, and they add a welcome crunchy bite. To enhance their flavor, they are often toasted before use. Only buy the amount of pine nuts you need because they do not keep well and quickly go rancid. They are sold shelled in small packages at many super-markets.

Pine nuts

FISH AND SHELLFISH

Pasta sauces made with fish or shellfish are quick and delicious. Fresh seafood is often the main ingredient, but there are a few other staples that are used over and over again.

Anchovies
Acciughe

The best anchovies are the salted ones that are packed in large cans. You see them on the counters of Italian markets, where they are sold loose by the pound. They must be rinsed, skinned and filleted before use, but

are plumper and more flavorsome than the fillets sold in jars and cans, so repay the effort. Anchovies are used in sauces for pasta all over Italy, but particularly in the hot South and in Sicily and Sardinia where strong and salty flavors are so popular. When chopped and heated gently with a little olive oil, they melt down to a creamy paste that is packed with flavor, so you only

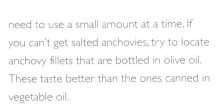

Anchovies in brine (left) and salt

need to use a small amount at a time. If you can't get salted anchovies, try to locate anchovy fillets that are bottled in olive oil. These taste better than the ones canned in vegetable oil.

Bottarga
Bottarga

This is the salted and air-dried roe of mullet or tuna. The best is the mullet, bottarga di muggine. It is a great delicacy in Sardinia, Sicily and the Veneto, where they like it grated over pasta or very thinly sliced as an antipasto with lemon juice and olive oil. You can buy bottarga quite easily at Italian markets, where it is kept in vacuum packs in the refrigerator. Mullet bottarga is delicate, moist and golden, like a pale, thin version of smoked cod's roe, and bears little resem-blance to tuna bottarga, which comes in a thick, dark block. For grating over pasta you

Tuna bottarga

Grated bottarga

Mullet bottarga

need only a small amount and it can be kept in the refrigerator for a long time (check the use-by date). You can also buy grated bottarga in small jars, but this product has a dry texture, and the flavor does not compare with that of freshly grated bottarga.

Clams
Vongole

In Italy, small fresh clams are frequently used in pasta sauces on the coast and in Sicily and Sardinia, but they are not always easy to get in other parts of the country or further afield. Names vary from one region and one country to another, but the name is not important; it is the size that counts. Small *vongole* cook quickly and have a

Fresh clams (left) and canned clams

tender texture and sweet flavor, which make them ideal for pasta sauces. Don't be tempted to buy the large ones. Some fishmongers sell frozen small clams, which are a good substitute for fresh; otherwise, you should buy the bottled shelled clams in natural juice that are sold at Italian markets Check labels carefully and don't buy the ones in vinegar or brine—these are intended for antipasto; their sharp flavor will spoil a pasta sauce. You can also buy bottled clams in their shells. These are packed in oil and, although intended primarily for antipasto, they also make an attractive garnish for a clam sauce.

Squid ink
Nero di seppia

If you want to color homemade pasta black, you can buy handy little sachets of squid ink at fishmongers and Italian markets and delicatessens. There is usually about 4 grams of ink in each sachet, and the sachets are sold in pairs. Two sachets are enough to color a 3-egg batch of pasta all'uovo.

Tuna
Tonno

For pasta sauces, use only best-quality canned tuna in olive oil, not the kind packed in vegetable oil, water or brine. Some large supermarkets sell it; otherwise you will have to go to an Italian market. The flesh of good-quality tuna is moist and meaty; inferior brands are watery and tasteless. The cost of a good can of tuna is generally less than that of fresh fish, poultry or meat, so no matter how much you spend on it, pasta with a tuna sauce will still be an inexpensive meal.

Canned tuna

VEGETABLES

Tomatoes are not the only vegetable to be used in sauces for pasta. Many others play an important part, either as a main ingredient or in a more minor role. Dried vegetables, such as porcini mushrooms, peppers and tomatoes, are used almost as often as fresh; valued for the intense flavour they impart to sauces and soups.

Dried grilled eggplant

Eggplant
Melanzane

Fresh eggplant is used as a main ingredient in many pasta sauces, especially in southern Italy, Sicily and Sardinia. Dried eggplant is not used as a substitute for fresh, but is added to fresh vegetables for its characteristic earthy flavor and meaty texture. Sold in cellophane packages, they are thin slices of eggplant that have been dried in the sun, and are a good pantry item, in that you can use as few or as many as you like. They need to be rehydrated in boiling water with a splash of white wine vinegar for 2 minutes before use, then drained and dried. They can then be snipped into strips and either added immediately to a simmering pasta sauce or fried first in olive oil.

Garlic
Aglio

Crushed, sliced and chopped garlic is used in many pasta sauces, but especially in those from the south of Italy, and whole garlic cloves are sometimes fried in olive oil at the beginning of cooking, then removed to leave behind a subtly flavored base for a sauce. One famous Roman pasta dish, *Spaghetti Aglio e Olio*, holds garlic in such high esteem that the sauce contains only two ingredients—garlic and olive oil—and in Rome they maintain it is the best cure for a hangover. The best Italian garlic is pink or purple tinged, with plump juicy cloves. In spring and early summer you can buy it fresh at some greengrocers and Italian markets

Garlic

This is the newly picked garlic that is sweet, moist and mild. As it dries out it becomes more pungent, so you need to adjust quantities accordingly. Buy garlic little and often so it neither sprouts green shoots nor becomes papery and dry.

Porcini mushrooms
Funghi porcini

Dried porcini (*boletus edulis*) are invaluable for the intense, musky aroma and flavor they impart to pasta sauces and soups. Italians use them all year round, not as a substitute for fresh porcini, but as a valued ingredient in its own right. A few dried porcini added to ordinary fresh mushrooms, for example, will give them the flavor of wild mushrooms. Don't buy cheap porcini, but look for packets containing large pale-colored pieces. Although they will seem expensive, a little goes a long way, and ¹/₂–1 oz is the most you will need in a recipe that serves 4–6 people.

Dried porcini mushrooms

Before use, dried porcini must be reconstituted in warm water for 15–20 minutes. Drain, rinse and squeeze dry, then slice or chop as required. Don't throw the soaking liquid away. Strain it to remove any grit and use it in soups and stocks, or add it to the water when cooking pasta to impart a mushroomy flavor—this is especially effective with fresh pasta.

Peppers
Peperoni

Sun-dried red peppers are sold in cellophane packets. They resemble sun-dried tomatoes, but their flavor is more peppery and piquant. They are used in the same way as tomatoes, to add a firm meaty bite to sauces and soups, especially those made with vegetables. Before use they should be rinsed under the cold tap, then dried and cut into thin strips or chopped.

Roasted peppers can be bought loose or in jars, packed in olive oil or brine. Although you can easily roast fresh peppers yourself when you need them, it is handy to keep a jar of commercially roasted peppers in the refrigerator. Just one piece of roasted pepper, sliced or chopped, will add a wonderful smoky flavor to pasta sauces, salads and soups. The best ones come from Italian markets where the peppers are grilled by hand and sold loose in extra virgin olive oil.

Dried peppers

Tomatoes
Pomodori

In summer, when fresh Italian plum tomatoes are ripe and full of flavor, it is wonderful to use these for sauce making, but at other times of the year you will get a much better flavor and color by using preserved tomatoes.

There are plenty of excellent tomato products to choose from, most of which come from southern Italy, where the hot sun ripens the tomatoes on the vine to an incomparable flavor.

Canned peeled plum tomatoes (*pomodori pelati*) come whole and chopped. Don't buy cheap brands; instead, opt for the top-quality Italian brands,

Bottled roasted peppers

Chopped canned plum tomatoes

Filetti di pomodoro (plum tomatoes in water and salt)

especially those that identify the tomatoes as San Marzano on the label. If you ask at your local Italian market, they will give you good advice. Plain chopped tomatoes are a good buy because they save you from having to chop them yourself, but they are slightly more expensive. If they are labeled polpa di pomodoro, they are likely to be very finely chopped or even crushed. Flavorings, such as garlic and herbs, should be added fresh, so don't buy chopped canned tomatoes containing these.

Filetti di pomodoro are sold in jars at good Italian markets and specialty food stores. These are plum tomatoes that have been halved or quartered and bottled *al*

Sun-dried tomato paste (left) and tomato paste

naturale in water and salt. They are about the nearest thing you can get to bottling tomatoes yourself at home, which Italians do in summer to preserve surplus tomatoes for winter use.

Crushed tomatoes come in many guises, and are a real boon for sauce making because they take all the hard work out of peeling, seeding and chopping. They are plum tomatoes that have been mechanically peeled and crushed, then sieved to remove the seeds. You can choose from passata, which is quite smooth, to polpa and sugocasa, which are quite chunky.

Bottles and jars of these products are good in that they allow you to see what you are buying. Cartons of very smooth passata take up less room and are lighter to carry; they are very popular with Italian cooks for making almost instant sauces.

Sun-dried tomatoes (*pomodori secchi*) are sold in two different forms—as dry pieces and in oil. Both types are piquant in flavor, but the dry pieces have a chewier texture than those in oil. Dried tomatoes are sold in cellophane packages and can be snipped directly into a long-cooking pasta sauce to intensify its tomato flavor, but generally they are best if softened in hot water for 2–3 hours before use. Sun-dried tomatoes in oil are sold in jars and can also be bought loose at some markets. For the best flavor, buy the ones in olive oil. They are soft and juicy and can be used as they are, either sliced or chopped, in sauces and salads.

Sun-dried tomato paste is a thick mixture of sun-dried tomatoes and olive oil. It can be used on its own as a quick sauce for pasta or added by the spoonful to tomato sauces to color and enrich them.

Although thick in texture, the flavor of sun-dried tomato paste is sweet and mild compared with tomato paste, and the color is paler.

Sun-dried tomatoes bottled in oil (top), and dry pieces

Tomato paste or concentrate (*concentrato di pomodoro*) is a very strong, thick paste made commercially from tomatoes, salt and citric acid. You can buy it in tubes, jars or cans, and its strength varies according to the manufacturer.

Clockwise from left, sugocasa, polpa and passata

Get to know the brand you like because some are quite bitter and sharp, and can overwhelm other flavors in a sauce. Only use tomato paste in small amounts or it may make a dish too acidic. A way to counteract acidity is to add a pinch or two or a lump of sugar.

Cheese and Cream

Italy's magnificent cheeses are famous all over the world, both as table cheeses and for their use in cooking. Many of them are used in sauces for pasta, in fillings for stuffed pasta and in baked dishes.

Fontina

Fontina

A mountain cheese from the Val d'Aosta in the northwest of Italy, fontina is used in baked pasta dishes, such as lasagne. It has superb melting qualities and a wonderful nutty, slightly sweet flavor. Some large supermarkets sell it; otherwise you can get it at specialty and cheese stores.

Gorgonzola

This blue-veined cheese comes from Lombardy. Although it is a table cheese, it melts quickly and well, so it is good in sauces and stuffed pasta, and its sharp flavor tastes very good combined with cream and leafy greens, such as spinach, sorrel and

Gorgonzola

herbs. Gorgonzola piccante is the very strong version, while dolcelatte is milder and sweeter, almost buttery.

Mascarpone

This is a full-fat cream cheese with a smooth silky texture, often used in pasta

Mascarpone

sauces instead of cream. It melts without curdling and has a slightly tangy flavor. It is widely available in tubs in at Italian markets and supermarkets.

Mozzarella

A soft white cheese, which is used in both salads and cooking, mozzarella melts quickly in hot sauces to serve with pasta, but must not be overcooked or it may become stringy. The whey should be drained off and discarded before the cheese is used. By

Mozzarella

tradition mozzarella should be made with buffalo's milk, but today it is often made with cow's or sheep's milk. Buy only the type that is swimming in whey in little bags—blocks of mozzarella are rubbery and tasteless. Mozzarella di bufala has the best texture and the most flavor, but it is more expensive than cow's or sheep's milk mozzarella and not so easy to find.

Parmesan

Grated Parmesan is most often used for sprinkling on pasta at the table, although it is also tossed with pasta after draining or added to sauces at the end of cooking. Genuine Parmigiano Reggiano has its name stamped on the rind and comes only from the area between Parma, Modena, Reggio-Emilia, Bologna and Mantua. It must be aged

for a minimum of 2 years, which is one of the reasons why it is so costly. Grana Padano is a similar, less expensive, cheese, which is used in the same way as Parmigiano Reggiano. Both are excellent melting cheeses, but Reggiano has a milder,

Pecorino (left) and Parmigiano Reggiano

less salty flavor and its texture is more flaky. Never buy these cheeses pre-grated. Buy them in a block and grate when you need, or shave into curls with a vegetable peeler.

Pecorino

This salty, hard sheep's milk cheese is called Pecorino Romano if it comes from Lazio, and Pecorino Sardo if it is Sardinian. It is used for grating in the same way as Parmesan, but because its flavor is sharper, it is used with the strong-tasting and spicy sauces associated with southern Italian and Sardinian cooking.

Ricotta salata (right) and ricotta

Enhancing Commercial Sauces

There are lots of bottled sauces for serving with pasta, ranging from chopped tomato sugocasa to classics, such as vongole, arrabbiata and alfredo , as well as unusual combinations of ingredients created by individual manufacturers. Generally speaking, it is best to stick to the Italian brands that are sold at supermarkets because these are the ones that Italians keep in their own pantries for times when they want to serve pasta at a moment's notice. You can use these sauces just as they are, but they will taste more homemade if you enliven them by adding something fresh.

Pesto

Both classic basil pesto and red pesto—made using sun-dried tomatoes—are available in jars and are useful pantry standbys. Grate a little fresh Parmesan cheese over the pasta before tossing with the pesto, and add a spoonful or two of extra virgin olive oil for a more fruity flavor. For a richer pesto sauce, add a spoonful or two of mascarpone cheese or cream (*below left*). Just before serving, sprinkle the pasta with more freshly grated Parmesan or with toasted pine nuts or shredded basil leaves.

Sugocasa/Chopped tomatoes

Add a little sun-dried tomato paste and/or a splash of red or white wine when heating up sugocasa, and season well with salt and ground black pepper. If you like a creamy tomato sauce, add up to ⅔ cup *panna da cucina*, heavy cream or crème fraîche. For a spicy kick, add a sprinkling of crushed dried red chiles. Finish the sauce with a small handful of shredded fresh basil or rocket, or use 1–2 tablespoons chopped fresh marjoram or oregano.

Arrabbiata

Strew a generous handful of finely shredded arugula leaves on top of the tossed pasta and sauce just before serving.

Alfredo

Stir a few spoonfuls of fresh cream into the sauce while it is heating up, then top with thin shavings of Parmesan cheese once the sauce and pasta have been tossed together.

Vongole

Add a splash of wine, some chopped fresh parsley and garlic. You can add all of these ingredients or just one or two of them. A few pitted and sliced black olives also look and taste good with a vongole sauce.

Ricotta

Fresh ricotta is a very soft white cheese, sold loose by the pound at Italian markets. It has superb melting qualities and is used in fillings for stuffed and baked pasta dishes, and for tossing with fresh raw vegetables, such as tomatoes, spinach and arugula, for uncooked sauces. Ricotta is low in fat and has a bland flavor, so it goes well with flavorful ingredients, such as herbs and garlic. Fresh ricotta does not keep well, so check before buying and only buy it if it is snowy white in color. If not, it is better to buy the ricotta sold in tubs—these are widely available at supermarkets. Ricotta salata is a hard, salted version of ricotta, cut from the block at Italian markets. It too is very white and low in fat. Ricotta salata is used for grating or crumbling over soups and pasta, especially in the south of Italy. You will find it saltier than Parmesan, Grana Padano or pecorino, so will need less.

Cream

Panna da cucina

For creamy pasta sauces, Italians use a type of cream called panna da cucina (cream for cooking). It is sold in little tubs, often joined together in pairs. Each tub contains a scant ½ cup, which is enough to make a

Panna da cucina

pasta sauce to serve 4 people. Panna da cucina is a long-life product, so it is well worth buying to keep in the pantry for making impromptu sauces. It is available in Italian markets.

Pasta Recipes

Pasta proves its enormous versatility in this section. With over 40 recipes to choose from, you won't need to look far for inspiration. Because there are very few hard-and-fast rules where pasta and sauces are concerned, you can call on your creative instincts and personalize them to your heart's content. Take these recipes as a starting point and create your very own unique dishes.

Each chapter has a range of recipes for every occasion. The Pasta Sauces chapter introduces sauces that are smooth and subtle and chunky and flavorsome, as well as cream sauces that are deliciously rich, and unbelievably quick to make.

The Quick and Healthy Dishes are great at any time of the day and call for the simplest of ingredients so whatever you are looking for, you are sure to find the ideal recipe. Vegetarian Meals offers a choice of classic and contemporary dishes that look and taste absolutely stunning and can be appreciated as much by meat-eaters as they can by vegetarians.

Lunch and Supper Dishes combines quick and tasty ideas with a range of slightly more complicated recipes that are ideal for serving to dinner party guests, while Baked Pasta Dishes provides a source of inspiration for family meals and suppers.

Try any of the wonderful recipes in these chapters and you'll be amazed and delighted at how easy pasta can be.

Pasta Sauces

When you think of pasta, your next thought is always of the sauce that is to accompany it. Tomato sauces, simple and uncooked or simmered for a longish while, are typical of southern Italy, while the northern Italians love cream sauce with pasta. Seafood sauces are often served with pasta along the Italian coastline and on the islands of Sicily and Sardinia, but they are very popular inland, too. Many meat sauces hail from the north of Italy, especially from the region of Emilia-Romagna, where both fresh meat and the famous hams, salami and sausages are enjoyed in abundance. The actual quantity of meat in the sauce is never very large, however, and the size of the pieces must be small.

Although some sauces are traditionally served with specific shapes of pasta, such as *Fettucine all'Alfredo*, there are no hard and fast rules as to which pasta should go with which sauce. Heavy sauces with large chunks are unlikely to go well with long, thin pasta as the chunks will slide off. Chunky sauces are better suited to short pasta shapes, and cream sauces tend to go well with fresh egg pasta.

La Pommarola

Fresh Tomato Sauce

THIS IS THE FAMOUS Neapolitan sauce that is made in summer when tomatoes are very ripe and sweet. It is very simple, so that nothing detracts from the flavor of the tomatoes themselves. It is served here with spaghetti, which is the traditional choice of pasta.

INGREDIENTS

1 1/2 pounds ripe Italian plum tomatoes
4 tablespoons olive oil
1 onion, finely chopped
12 ounces fresh or dried spaghetti
1 small handful fresh basil leaves
salt and ground black pepper
coarsely shaved Parmesan cheese, to serve
Serves 4

1 With a sharp knife, cut a cross in the bottom (flower) end of each tomato. Bring a medium saucepan of water to a boil and remove from heat. Plunge a few of the tomatoes into the water, set aside for 30 seconds or so, then lift them out with a slotted spoon. Repeat with the remaining tomatoes, then peel off the skin and coarsely chop the flesh.

2 Heat the oil in a large saucepan, add the onion and cook over low heat, stirring frequently, for about 5 minutes until softened and lightly colored. Add the tomatoes, with salt and pepper to taste, bring to a simmer, then turn the heat down to low and cover the pan. Cook, stirring occasionally, for 30–40 minutes or until thick.

3 Meanwhile, cook the pasta according to the instructions on the package. Shred the basil leaves finely.

4 Remove the sauce from heat, stir in the basil and taste for seasoning. Drain the pasta, turn it into a warmed bowl, pour the sauce over and toss well. Serve immediately, with shaved Parmesan passed separately.

COOK'S TIPS

• If good plum tomatoes are not available, substitute large ripe tomatoes which give excellent results.
• In Italy, cooks often make this sauce in bulk in the summer months and freeze it for later use. Let it cool, then freeze in usable quantities in rigid contailes. Thaw before reheating.

VARIATIONS

Some Neapolitan cooks add a little crushed garlic with the onion and some use chopped fresh oregano or Italian parsley with the basil; it is a matter of personal taste.

Fettuccine all'Alfredo
Alfredo's Fettuccine

THIS SIMPLE RECIPE WAS invented by a Roman restaurateur called Alfredo, who became famous for serving it with a gold fork and spoon.

INGREDIENTS

1/4 cup butter

scant 1 cup panna da cucina or
    heavy cream

2/3 cup freshly grated Parmesan cheese,
    plus extra to serve

12 ounces fresh fettuccine

salt and ground black pepper

Serves 4

1 Melt the butter in a large saucepan or skillet. Add the cream and bring it to a boil. Simmer for 5 minutes, stirring, then add the Parmesan, with salt and pepper to taste, and turn off the heat under the pan.

2 Bring a large pot of salted water to a boil. Drop in the pasta all at once and quickly bring back to a boil, stirring occasionally. Cook until *al dente*: 2–3 minutes, or according to the instructions on the package. Drain well.

3 Turn on the heat under the pan of cream to low, add the pasta all at once and toss until it is coated in the sauce. Taste for seasoning. Serve immediately, with extra grated Parmesan passed separately.

COOK'S TIPS

• *With so few ingredients, it is particularly important to use only the best-quality ones for this dish to be a success. Use good unsalted butter and top-quality Parmesan cheese. The best is Parmigiano-Reggiano—available from Italian markets—which has its name stamped on the rind. Grate it only just before using.*

• *Fresh fettuccine is traditional, so either make it yourself or buy it from an Italian delicatessen. If you cannot get fettuccine, you can use tagliatelle instead.*

Agnolotti alla Salsa di Vodka

Meat-filled Agnolotti with Vodka Sauce

DAINTY HALF MOON SHAPES are filled with spiced ground meat and bacon and served with a cream and blue-cheese sauce spiked with vodka. This is a very special dish for a dinner party first course.

INGREDIENTS

1 recipe Pasta with Eggs
freshly grated Parmesan cheese, to serve

For the filling
1 tablespoon olive oil
3 ounces pancetta, lean bacon or ham,
*   finely diced*
9 ounces ground pork or veal
2 garlic cloves, crushed
good pinch of ground cinnamon
1/2 cup red wine
4 tablespoons chopped fresh Italian parsley
1 small egg
salt and ground black pepper

For the sauce
1/4 cup butter
1 cup panna da cucina or heavy cream
4 ounces Gorgonzola cheese, diced
3 tablespoons vodka
Serves 6–8

1 Make the filling. Heat the oil in a medium saucepan, add the pancetta, bacon or ham and stir-fry for a few minutes until lightly colored. Add the ground pork, the garlic, cinnamon and salt and pepper to taste and cook gently for 5–6 minutes, stirring frequently and breaking up any lumps.

2 Pour in the wine and stir well to mix, then simmer gently, stirring occasionally, for 15–20 minutes, until the meat is cooked and quite dry. Transfer the meat to a bowl with a slotted spoon and set aside to cool.

3 Add the parsley and egg to the meat mixture and stir well to mix.

4 Using a pasta machine, roll out one-quarter of the pasta into a 36-inch–40-inch strip. Cut the strip with a sharp knife into two 18–20-inch lengths (you can do this during rolling if the strip gets too long to manage).

5 Using a teaspoon, put 8–10 little mounds of the filling along one side of one of the pasta strips, spacing them evenly. Brush a little water around each mound, then fold the plain side of the pasta strip over the filling.

6 Starting from the folded edge, press down gently with your fingertips around each mound, pushing the air out at the unfolded edge.

7 Using only half of a 2-inch fluted round ravioli or biscuit cutter, cut around each mound of filling to make a half-moon shape. The folded edge should be the straight edge. If you like, press the cut edges of the agnolotti with the tines of a fork to give a decorative effect.

8 Put the agnolotti on floured dish towels, spreading them out in a single layer, so that they don't stick together. Sprinkle them lightly with flour and allow to dry while repeating the process with the remaining pasta, to get 64–80 agnolotti altogether.

9 Drop the agnolotti into a large pot of salted boiling water, bring back to a boil and boil for 4–5 minutes.

10 Meanwhile, make the sauce. Melt the butter in a medium saucepan, add the cream and cheese and heat through, stirring, until the cheese has melted. Add the vodka, season to taste with pepper and stir well to mix.

11 Drain the agnolotti and divide them among six or eight warmed bowls. Spoon the sauce over them and sprinkle liberally with grated Parmesan. Serve immediately.

VARIATIONS

• Instead of the pancetta, bacon or ham, you could use a spicy salami for the agnolotti filling. Buy the salami in one very thick piece, peel off the skin, then chop the salami finely.

• Agnolotti are also often made with prosciutto crudo, which gives them a more delicate flavor than the streaky pancetta.

COOK'S TIP

Gorgonzola is a sharp-tasting blue Italian cheese with a soft and creamy consistency. Gorgonzola piccante is a particularly strong variety, while gorgonzola dolce—better known as dolcelatte—is creamier and less sharp in flavor. Supermarkets, specialty cheese stores and markets usually sell both types of Gorgonzola.

Tortellini con Prosciutto
Tortellini with Ham

THIS IS A VERY EASY RECIPE that can be made quickly from pantry ingredients. It is therefore ideal for an after-work supper.

INGREDIENTS

9-ounce package tortellini alla carne
   (meat-filled tortellini)
2 tablespoons olive oil
1 small onion, finely chopped
4 ounces cooked ham, diced
*²/3 cup strained crushed Italian
   plum tomatoes*
*scant ¹/2 cup panna da cucina or
   heavy cream*
*generous 1 cup freshly grated
   Parmesan cheese*
salt and ground black pepper
Serves 4

1 Cook the pasta according to the instructions on the package.

2 Meanwhile, heat the oil in a large skillet or saucepan, add the onion and cook over low heat, stirring frequently, for about 5 minutes, until softened. Add the ham and cook, stirring occasionally, until it darkens.

3 Add the strained crushed tomatoes. Fill the empty carton with water and pour it into the pan. Stir well, then add salt and pepper to taste. Bring to a boil, lower the heat and simmer the sauce for a few minutes, stirring occasionally, until it has reduced slightly. Stir in the cream. Drain the pasta well and add it to the sauce.

4 Add a handful of grated Parmesan to the pan. Stir, toss well and taste for seasoning. Serve in warmed bowls, topped with the remaining Parmesan.

COOK'S TIP

Cartons of strained crushed tomatoes are handy for making quick sauces.

Ragù al Vino Rosso
Bolognese Sauce with Red Wine

THIS IS A VERSATILE meat sauce. You can toss it with freshly cooked pasta—the quantity here is enough for 1 pound tagliatelle, spaghetti or a short pasta shape such as penne or fusilli—or alternatively you can layer it in a baked dish like lasagne.

INGREDIENTS

1 medium onion
1 small carrot
1 celery stalk
2 garlic cloves
3 tablespoons olive oil
14 ounces ground beef
¹/2 cup red wine
scant 1 cup tomato sauce
1 tablespoon tomato purée
1 teaspoon dried oregano
1 tablespoon chopped fresh Italian parsley
1¹/2 cups beef stock
8 small plum tomatoes (optional)
salt and ground black pepper
Serves 4–6

1 Chop all the vegetables finely, either in a food processor or by hand. Heat the oil in a large saucepan, add the chopped vegetable mixture and cook over low heat, stirring frequently, for 5–7 minutes.

2 Add the ground beef and cook for 5 minutes, stirring frequently and breaking up any lumps in the meat with a wooden spoon.

3 Stir in the wine and mix well. Cook for 1–2 minutes, then add the tomato sauce, tomato purée, herbs and 4 tablespoons of the stock. Season with salt and pepper to taste. Stir well and bring to a boil.

4 Cover the pan, and cook over low heat for 30–40 minutes, stirring, adding more stock as necessary. Add the tomatoes, if using, and simmer for 5–10 minutes more. Taste for seasoning and toss with hot, freshly cooked pasta, or use in baked pasta dishes.

Vermicelli alla Napoletana

Vermicelli with Clam Sauce

THIS RECIPE TAKES ITS name from the city of Naples, where both fresh tomato sauce and seafood are traditionally served with vermicelli. Here the two are combined to make a very tasty dish.

INGREDIENTS

2¼ pounds fresh hard-shell clams

1 cup dry white wine

2 garlic cloves, bruised

1 large handful fresh Italian parsley

2 tablespoons olive oil

1 small onion, finely chopped

8 ripe Italian plum tomatoes, peeled, seeded and finely chopped

½–1 fresh red chile, seeded and finely chopped

12 ounces vermicelli

salt and ground black pepper

Serves 4

1 Scrub the clams thoroughly under cold running water and discard any that are open or that do not close when sharply tapped against the work surface.

2 Pour the wine into a large saucepan, add the garlic cloves and half the parsley, then the clams. Cover tightly with the lid and bring to a boil over high heat. Cook for about 5 minutes, shaking the pan frequently, until the clams have opened.

3 Turn the clams into a large colander set over a bowl and let the liquid drain through. Set aside the clams until cool enough to handle, then remove about two-thirds of them from their shells, pouring the clam liquid into the bowl of cooking liquid. Discard any clams that have failed to open. Set both shelled and unshelled clams aside, keeping the unshelled clams warm in a bowl covered with a lid.

4 Heat the oil in a saucepan, add the onion and cook gently, stirring frequently, for about 5 minutes until softened and lightly colored. Add the tomatoes, then strain in the clam cooking liquid. Add the chile and salt and pepper to taste.

5 Bring to a boil, half cover the pan and simmer gently for 15–20 minutes. Meanwhile, cook the pasta according to the package instructions. Chop the remaining parsley finely.

6 Add the shelled clams to the tomato sauce, stir well and heat through very gently for 2–3 minutes.

7 Drain the cooked pasta well and turn it into a warmed bowl. Taste the sauce for seasoning, then pour the sauce over the pasta and toss everything together well. Garnish with the reserved clams, sprinkle the parsley over the pasta and serve immediately.

Penne with Chicken, Broccoli and Cheese

THE COMBINATION OF BROCCOLI, garlic and Gorgonzola is very good, and goes especially well with chicken.

INGREDIENTS

scant 1 cup broccoli florets, divided into
    tiny sprigs
1/4 cup butter
2 skinless chicken breast fillets, cut into
    thin strips
2 garlic cloves, crushed
3 1/2 cups penne
1/2 cup dry white wine
scant 1 cup panna da cucina or
    heavy cream
3 1/2 ounces Gorgonzola cheese, rind
    removed and diced small
salt and ground black pepper
freshly grated Parmesan cheese, to serve

Serves 4

1 Plunge the broccoli into a saucepan of boiling salted water. Bring back to a boil and boil for 2 minutes, then drain in a colander and refresh under cold running water. Shake well to remove the surplus water and set aside to drain completely.

2 Melt the butter in a large skillet or saucepan, add the chicken and garlic, with salt and pepper to taste, and stir well. Fry over medium heat for 3 minutes or until the chicken becomes white. Meanwhile, start cooking the pasta according to the instructions on the package.

3 Pour the wine and cream over the chicken mixture in the pan, stir to mix, then simmer, stirring occasionally, for about 5 minutes, until the sauce has reduced and thickened. Add the broccoli, increase the heat and toss to heat it through and mix it with the chicken. Taste for seasoning.

4 Drain the pasta and add it to the sauce. Add the Gorgonzola and toss well. Serve with grated Parmesan.

VARIATION

Use leeks instead of broccoli if you prefer. Fry them with the chicken.

Quick & Healthy Pasta Dishes

Devoted to quick and healthy recipes, this chapter proves the point that pasta not only looks and tastes good, but that it is quick to prepare and nutritionally sound. The dishes in this chapter range from the traditional to the contemporary. Some consist of little more than a handful of fresh ingredients tossed with hot pasta, while others rely on store cupboard faithfuls, such as tomatoes and tuna fish. Other recipes can be prepared in advance and eaten cold with salad.

All the recipes are tried and tested but it is always good to remember that half the fun of making pasta is in inventing your own combinations. The key to success lies in the quality of the ingredients, and only the best will do. This goes for the pasta as much as anything else. Buy Italian brands of pasta to be sure of good texture and taste. Additive-free and packed with nutrients, pasta makes the perfect foundation for a healthy meal.

Frittata di Vermicelli

Vermicelli Omelette

A FRITTATA IS A FLAT BAKED omelette. Here it is made with vegetables and herbs, but you can put anything you like in it. Ham, sausage, salami, chicken, mushrooms, zucchini and eggplant are just a few suggestions, or you could simply add mixed herbs. Frittata is absolutely delicious cold. Cut into wedges, it is excellent food for picnics.

INGREDIENTS

2 ounces vermicelli

6 eggs

4 tablespoons panna da cucina or
    heavy cream

1 handful fresh basil leaves, shredded

1 handful fresh Italian parsley, chopped

1 cup freshly grated Parmesan cheese

2 tablespoons butter

1 tablespoon olive oil

1 onion, finely sliced

3 large pieces bottled roasted red pepper,
    drained, rinsed, dried and cut into strips

1 garlic clove, crushed

salt and ground black pepper

arugula leaves, to serve

Serves 4–6

1 | Preheat the oven to 375°F. Cook the pasta in a pot of salted boiling water for 8 minutes.

2 Meanwhile, break the eggs into a bowl and add the cream and herbs. Whisk in about two-thirds of the grated Parmesan and add salt and pepper to taste.

3 Drain the pasta well and allow to cool; snip it into short lengths with scissors. Add to the egg mixture and whisk again. Set aside.

4 Melt the butter in the oil in a large, ovenproof nonstick frying pan. Add the onion and cook gently, stirring frequently, for 5 minutes until softened. Add the peppers and garlic.

5 Pour the egg and pasta mixture into the pan and stir well. Cook over low to medium heat, without stirring, for 3–5 minutes or until the frittata is just set underneath. Sprinkle over the remaining Parmesan and bake in the oven for 5 minutes or until set. Before serving, allow to stand for at least 5 minutes. Cut into wedges and serve warm or cold, with arugula.

Farfalle al Sugo di Tonno
Farfalle with Tuna

A QUICK AND SIMPLE DISH that makes
a good weekday supper if you
have canned tomatoes and tuna in
the pantry.

INGREDIENTS

2 tablespoons olive oil
1 small onion, finely chopped
1 garlic clove, finely chopped
1 can (14 ounces) chopped Italian
    plum tomatoes
3 tablespoons dry white wine
8–10 pitted black olives, cut into rings
2 teaspoons chopped fresh oregano or
    1 teaspoon dried oregano, plus extra fresh
    oregano to garnish
3¹/2 cups farfalle
1 can (6 ounces) tuna in olive oil
salt and ground black pepper
Serves 4

1 Heat the olive oil in a medium skillet
or saucepan, add the onion and garlic
and fry gently for 2–3 minutes, until
the onion is soft and golden.

2 Add the plum tomatoes and bring
to a boil, then add the white wine
and simmer for a minute or so. Stir in
the olives and oregano, with salt and
pepper to taste, then cover and cook
for 20–25 minutes, stirring from time
to time.

3 Meanwhile, cook the pasta in a
large pot of salted boiling water
according to the instructions
on the package.

4 Drain the canned tuna and flake
it with a fork. Add the tuna to the
sauce with about 4 tablespoons of the
water used for cooking the pasta. Taste
and adjust the seasoning.

5 Drain the cooked pasta well and
turn it into a warmed large serving
bowl. Pour the tuna sauce over the top
and toss to mix. Serve immediately,
garnished with sprigs of oregano.

Rigatoni ai Funghi di Bosco

Rigatoni with Wild Mushrooms

THIS IS A GOOD SAUCE to make from pantry ingredients because it doesn't rely on anything fresh, apart from the fresh herbs.

INGREDIENTS

2 1/2-ounce packages dried porcini
   mushrooms
3/4 cup warm water
2 tablespoons olive oil
2 shallots, finely chopped
2 garlic cloves, crushed
a few sprigs of fresh marjoram, leaves
   stripped and finely chopped, plus extra
   to garnish
1 handful fresh Italian parsley, chopped
2 tablespoons butter, diced
1 can (14 ounces) chopped Italian
   plum tomatoes
3 1/2 cups rigatoni
1/3 cup freshly grated Parmesan cheese,
   plus extra to serve
salt and ground black pepper
Serves 4–6

1 Put the dried mushrooms in a bowl, pour the warm water over and soak for 15–20 minutes. Turn into a fine sieve set over a bowl and squeeze the mushrooms to release as much liquid as possible. Reserve the mushrooms and the strained liquid.

2 Heat the oil in a medium skillet and fry the shallots, garlic and herbs over low heat, stirring frequently, for about 5 minutes. Add the mushrooms and butter and stir until the butter has melted. Season well.

3 Stir in the tomatoes and the reserved liquid from the soaked mushrooms. Bring to a boil, then cover, lower the heat and simmer for about 20 minutes, stirring occasionally. Meanwhile, cook the pasta according to the instructions on the package.

4 Taste the sauce for seasoning. Drain the pasta, reserving some of the cooking water, and turn it into a warmed large bowl. Add the sauce and the grated Parmesan and toss to mix. Add a little cooking water if you prefer a runnier sauce. Serve immediately, garnished with marjoram and with more Parmesan passed separately.

VARIATIONS

• *If you have a bottle of wine open, add a splash with the canned tomatoes.*
• *For a richer sauce, add a few spoonfuls of* panna da cucina, *cream or mascarpone to the sauce just before serving.*

Strozzapreti ai Fiori di Zucca

Strozzapreti with Zucchini Flowers

THIS PRETTY, SUMMERY DISH is strewn with zucchini flowers, but you can make it even if you don't have the flowers. In Italy, bunches of fresh zucchini flowers are a common sight on vegetable stalls in summer, and are frequently used for stuffing and cooking.

INGREDIENTS

1/4 cup butter

2 tablespoons extra virgin olive oil

1 small onion, thinly sliced

7 ounces small zucchini, cut into
 thin julienne

1 garlic clove, crushed

2 teaspoons finely chopped fresh marjoram

3 cups strozzapreti

1 large handful zucchini flowers,
 thoroughly washed and dried

salt and ground black pepper

thin shavings of Parmesan cheese, to serve

Serves 4

1 Heat the butter and half the olive oil in a medium skillet or saucepan, add the sliced onion and cook gently, stirring frequently, for about 5 minutes until softened. Add the zucchini to the pan and sprinkle with the crushed garlic, chopped marjoram and salt and pepper to taste. Cook for 5–8 minutes until the zucchini have softened but are not colored, turning them over from time to time.

2 Meanwhile, cook the pasta in a large pot of salted boiling water according to the package instructions.

3 Set aside a few whole zucchini flowers for the garnish, then coarsely shred the rest and add them to the zucchini mixture. Stir to mix and taste for seasoning.

4 Drain the pasta, turn it into a warmed large bowl and add the remaining oil. Toss, add the zucchini mixture and toss again. Top with Parmesan and the reserved flowers.

COOK'S TIP

Strozzapreti or "priest stranglers" are a special kind of short pasta shape from Modena. You can buy packages of them in Italian markets, or use gemelli, a similar kind of twisted pasta.

Tagliatelle Tricolore

Three-color Tagliatelle

ZUCCHINI AND CARROTS are cut into delicate ribbons so that when they are cooked and tossed with tagliatelle they look like colored pasta. Serve as a side dish, or sprinkle with freshly grated Parmesan cheese for a light first course or vegetarian main course.

INGREDIENTS

2 large zucchini

2 large carrots

9 ounces fresh egg tagliatelle

4 tablespoons extra virgin olive oil

flesh of 2 roasted garlic cloves, plus extra
    roasted garlic cloves, to serve (optional)

salt and ground black pepper

Serves 4

1 With a vegetable peeler, cut the zucchini and carrots into long thin ribbons. Bring a large pot of salted water to a boil, then add the zucchini and carrot ribbons. Bring the water back to a boil and boil for 30 seconds, then drain and set aside.

2 Cook the pasta according to the instructions on the package.

3 Drain the pasta and return it to the pot. Add the vegetable ribbons, oil, garlic and salt and pepper and toss over medium to high heat until the pasta and vegetables are glistening with oil. Serve immediately, with extra roasted garlic, if you like.

COOK'S TIP

To roast garlic, put a whole head of garlic on a lightly oiled baking sheet. Place in a 350°F oven and roast for about 30 minutes. Remove the garlic from the oven and set aside. When cool enough to handle, dig out the flesh from the cloves with the point of a knife. If you don't want to go to the trouble of roasting garlic, you can use crushed raw garlic but the flavor will be stronger.

Rigatoni con Sugo di Pomodoro Invernale

Rigatoni with Winter Tomato Sauce

IN WINTER, WHEN FRESH tomatoes are not at their best, this is the sauce the Italians make. Canned tomatoes combined with *soffritto* (the sautéed mixture of chopped onion, carrot, celery and garlic) and herbs give a better flavor than winter tomatoes.

INGREDIENTS

1 onion

1 carrot

1 celery stalk

4 tablespoons olive oil

1 garlic clove, thinly sliced

a few leaves each fresh basil, thyme and
  oregano or marjoram

2 (14-ounce) cans chopped Italian
  plum tomatoes

1 tablespoon sun-dried tomato paste

1 teaspoon granulated sugar

6 tablespoons dry red or
  white wine (optional)

3 cups rigatoni

salt and ground black pepper

coarsely shaved Parmesan cheese, to serve

Serves 6–8

1 Chop the onion, carrot and celery stalk finely, either in a food processor or by hand.

2 Heat the olive oil in a medium saucepan, add the garlic slices and stir over very low heat for 1–2 minutes.

3 Add the chopped vegetables and the fresh herbs. Cook over low heat, stirring frequently, for 5–7 minutes until the vegetables have softened and are lightly colored.

4 Add the canned tomatoes, tomato paste and sugar, then stir in the wine, if using. Add salt and pepper to taste. Bring to a boil, stirring, then lower the heat to a gentle simmer. Cook, uncovered, for about 45 minutes, stirring occasionally.

5 Cook the pasta according to the instructions on the package. Drain it and turn it into a warmed bowl. Taste the sauce for seasoning, pour the sauce over the pasta and toss well. Serve immediately, with shavings of Parmesan passed separately. If you like, garnish with extra chopped herbs.

Fusilli con Salsa di Pomodori all'Aceto Balsamico

Fusilli with Tomato and Balsamic Vinegar Sauce

THIS IS A MODERN CAL-ITAL recipe (Californian/Italian). The intense, sweet-sour flavor of balsamic vinegar gives a pleasant kick to a sauce made with canned tomatoes.

INGREDIENTS

2 cans (14-ounce) chopped Italian
   plum tomatoes
2 pieces of drained sun-dried tomato in
   olive oil, thinly sliced
2 garlic cloves, crushed
3 tablespoons olive oil
1 teaspoon granulated sugar
3 cups fresh or dried fusilli
3 tablespoons balsamic vinegar
salt and ground black pepper
coarsely shaved pecorino cheese and
   arugula salad, to serve

Serves 6–8

1 Put the canned and sun-dried tomatoes in a medium saucepan with the garlic, olive oil and sugar. Add salt and pepper to taste. Bring to a boil, stirring. Lower the heat and simmer for about 30 minutes until reduced.

2 Meanwhile, cook the pasta in salted boiling water according to the instructions on the package.

3 Add the balsamic vinegar to the sauce and stir to mix evenly. Cook for 1–2 minutes, then remove from heat and taste for seasoning.

4 Drain the pasta and turn it into a warmed bowl. Pour the sauce over the pasta and toss well. Serve immediately, with arugula salad and the shaved pecorino handed separately.

Linguine con Pesto di Pomodori Secchi

Linguine with Sun-dried Tomato Pesto

TOMATO PESTO WAS ONCE a rarity, but is becoming increasingly popular. To make it, sun-dried tomatoes are used instead of basil. The result is absolutely delicious.

INGREDIENTS

1/3 cup pine nuts

1/3 cup freshly grated Parmesan cheese

1/2 cup sun-dried tomatoes
    in olive oil

1 garlic clove, coarsely chopped

4 tablespoons olive oil

12 ounces fresh or dried linguine

ground black pepper

coarsely shaved Parmesan cheese, to serve

basil leaves, to garnish

Serves 4

3 With the machine running, gradually add the olive oil through the feeder tube until it has all been incorporated evenly and the ingredients have formed a smooth-looking paste.

4 Cook the pasta according to the package instructions. Drain well, reserving a little of the cooking water. Turn the pasta into a warmed bowl, add the pesto and a few spoonfuls of the hot water and toss well. Serve immediately, garnish with basil leaves. Pass shavings of Parmesan separately.

1 Put the pine nuts in a small nonstick frying pan and toss over low to medium heat for 1–2 minutes or until the nuts are lightly toasted and golden.

2 Put the nuts in a food processor. Add the Parmesan, sun-dried tomatoes and garlic, with pepper to taste. Process until finely chopped.

COOK'S TIP

You can make this pesto up to 2 days in advance and keep it in a bowl in the refrigerator until ready to use. Pour a thin film of olive oil over the pesto in the bowl, then cover the bowl tightly with plastic wrap to prevent the pesto from flavoring other foods in the refrigerator.

Vegetarian Meals

Pasta started its life as the food of the poor and vegetables were often the only other ingredients that they could afford. It is little wonder, therefore, that pasta recipes are such a haven for vegetarians and vegetable-lovers today. Served with a vegetable sauce, pasta truly comes into its own. However, a vegetarian pasta dish need not just mean pasta served with vegetables. Some of the most delicious recipes consist simply of butter, olive oil, garlic, herbs, cheese and freshly ground black pepper.

Many of the recipes in this chapter are made from the simplest of ingredients and can be cooked in a very short time, making them perfect for quick afterwork suppers. Other recipes may take a little longer to prepare but are sure to impress a vegetarian guest. This chapter provides a choice of some of the most tempting vegetarian combinations, including freshly cooked pasta tossed with roasted vegetables, stuffed pastas, cream sauces and pasta baked in the oven to create a vegetarian pie. Whether you are a vegetarian or a confirmed meat eater, these recipes are sure to inspire and delight.

Conchiglie con Verdure Arrostite

Conchiglie with Roasted Vegetables

NOTHING COULD BE SIMPLER—or more delicious—than tossing freshly cooked pasta with roasted vegetables. The flavor is superb.

INGREDIENTS

1 red bell pepper, seeded and cut into
   $^{1}/_{2}$-inch squares
1 yellow or orange bell pepper, seeded and
   cut into $^{1}/_{2}$-inch squares
1 small eggplant, coarsely diced
2 zucchini, coarsely diced
5 tablespoons extra virgin olive oil
1 tablespoon chopped fresh
   Italian parsley
1 teaspoon dried oregano or marjoram
9 ounces baby Italian plum tomatoes,
   cored and halved lengthwise
2 garlic cloves, coarsely chopped
3–3$^{1}/_{2}$ cups conchiglie
salt and ground black pepper
4–6 fresh marjoram or oregano sprigs,
   to garnish
Serves 4–6

1 Preheat the oven to 375°F. Rinse the prepared peppers, eggplant and zucchini in a strainer or colander under cold running water, drain, then turn the vegetables into a large roasting pan.

2 Pour 3 tablespoons of the olive oil over the vegetables and sprinkle with the fresh and dried herbs. Add salt and pepper to taste and stir well. Roast for about 30 minutes, stirring two or three times.

3 Stir the halved tomatoes and chopped garlic into the vegetable mixture, then roast for 20 minutes more, stirring once or twice. Meanwhile, cook the pasta according to the instructions on the package.

4 Drain the pasta and turn it into a warmed bowl. Add the roasted vegetables and the remaining oil and toss well. Serve the pasta and vegetables hot in warmed bowls, sprinkling each portion with a few herb flowers.

COOK'S TIP

Pasta and roasted vegetables are very good served cold, so if you have any of this dish left over, cover it tightly with plastic wrap, chill in the refrigerator overnight and serve it the next day as a salad. It would also make a particularly good salad to take on a picnic.

Orecchiette con la Rucola

Orecchiette with Arugula

THIS HEARTY DISH IS FROM PUGLIA in the south-east of Italy. Serve it as a main course with country bread. Some specialty markets and super-markets sell a farmhouse-style Italian loaf called *pugliese*, which would be the most appropriate.

INGREDIENTS

3 tablespoons olive oil
1 small onion, finely chopped
11 ounces canned chopped Italian plum
   tomatoes or tomato sauce
$1/2$ teaspoon dried oregano
pinch of cayenne pepper
2 tablespoons red or white wine (optional)
2 potatoes, total weight about
   7 ounces, diced
$2^3/4$ cups orecchiette
2 garlic cloves, finely chopped
5 ounces arugula leaves, stalks
   removed, shredded
scant $1/2$ cup ricotta cheese
salt and ground black pepper
freshly grated pecorino cheese, to serve

Serves 4–6

1 Heat 1 tablespoon of the olive oil in a medium saucepan, add half the finely chopped onion and cook gently, stirring frequently, for about 5 minutes, until softened. Add the canned tomatoes or tomato sauce, oregano and cayenne pepper to the onion. Pour the wine over, if using, and add a little salt and pepper to taste. Cover the pan and simmer for about 15 minutes, stirring occasionally.

2 Bring a large pot of salted water to a boil. Add the potatoes and pasta. Stir well and let the water return to a boil. Lower the heat and simmer for 15 minutes, or according to the instructions on the package, until the pasta is cooked.

3 Heat the remaining oil in a large skillet or saucepan, add the rest of the onion and the garlic and fry for 2–3 minutes, stirring occasionally. Add the arugula, toss over the heat for about 2 minutes, until wilted, then stir in the tomato sauce and the ricotta. Mix well.

4 Drain the pasta and potatoes, add both to the pan of sauce and toss to mix. Taste for seasoning and serve immediately in warmed bowls, with grated pecorino handed separately.

COOK'S TIP

Orecchiette are always slightly chewy. When making this dish it is traditional to cook them in the same pan as the potatoes, but if you are not sure of getting the timing right, cook them separately.

Ravioli di Magro

Spinach and Ricotta Ravioli

THE LITERAL TRANSLATION OF *ravioli di magro* is lean ravioli. It is used to describe meatless ravioli, usually those with a spinach and ricotta filling. *Ravioli di magro* are served on Christmas Eve, a time when meat-filled pasta should not be eaten.

INGREDIENTS

1 recipe Pasta with Eggs
freshly grated Parmesan cheese, to serve

For the filling

3 tablespoons butter
6 ounces fresh spinach leaves, trimmed, washed and shredded
scant 1 cup ricotta cheese
1/3 cup freshly grated Parmesan cheese
nutmeg
1 small egg
salt and ground black pepper

For the sauce

1/4 cup butter
1 cup panna da cucina or heavy cream
2/3 cup freshly grated Parmesan cheese

Serves 8

1 Make the filling. Melt the butter in a medium saucepan, add the spinach and salt and pepper to taste and cook over medium heat for 5–8 minutes, stirring frequently, until the spinach is wilted and tender. Increase the heat to high and stir until the water boils off and the spinach is quite dry.

2 Tip the spinach into a bowl and set aside until cold, then add the ricotta, grated Parmesan and freshly grated nutmeg to taste. Beat well to mix, taste for seasoning, then add the egg and beat well again.

3 Using a pasta machine, roll out one-quarter of the pasta into a 36-inch–40-inch strip. Cut the strip with a sharp knife into two 18–20-inch lengths (you can do this during rolling if the strip gets too long to manage).

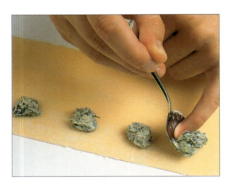

4 Using a teaspoon, put 10–12 little mounds of the filling along one side of one of the pasta strips, spacing them evenly. Brush a little water around each mound, then fold the plain side of the pasta strip over the filling.

5 Starting from the folded edge, press down gently with your fingertips around each mound of filling, pushing the air out at the unfolded edge. Sprinkle lightly with flour.

6 With a fluted pasta wheel, cut along each long side, then in between each mound to make small square shapes.

7 Put the ravioli on floured dish towels, sprinkle lightly with flour and allow to dry while repeating the process with the remaining pasta, to get 80–96 ravioli altogether.

8 Drop the ravioli into a large pot of salted boiling water, bring back to a boil and boil for 4–5 minutes.

9 Meanwhile, make the sauce. Gently heat the butter, cream and Parmesan in a medium saucepan until the butter and Parmesan have melted.

I0 Increase the heat and simmer for a minute or two until the sauce is slightly reduced, then add salt and pepper to taste.

II Drain the ravioli and divide them equally among 8 warmed large bowls. Drizzle the sauce over them and serve immediately, sprinkled with grated Parmesan.

VARIATION

If you prefer, serve the ravioli with sizzling sage butter. Melt $^1/4$ cup butter in a small pan, add a handful of fresh sage leaves and stir constantly over medium to high heat until sizzling. This will be slightly less rich than the cream sauce suggested here.

COOK'S TIP

To keep the pasta from sticking when working with it, lightly flour the work surface and your cutting tools and use more flour as necessary.

Conchiglie Ripiene

Stuffed Shells

THIS MAKES AN EXCELLENT dinner party first course for six, or a vegetarian main course for four, in which case you should fill 20 shells, rather than 18; there will be plenty of filling.

INGREDIENTS

18 large pasta shells for stuffing

2 tablespoons butter

1 small onion, finely chopped

10 ounces fresh spinach leaves, trimmed, washed and shredded

1 garlic clove, crushed

1 envelope of saffron powder

nutmeg

generous 1 cup ricotta cheese

1 egg

1 recipe Winter Tomato Sauce

2/3 cup dry white wine, vegetable stock or water

scant 1/2 cup panna da cucina or heavy cream

2/3 cup freshly grated Parmesan cheese

salt and ground black pepper

Serves 6

1 Preheat the oven to 375°F. Bring a large pot of salted water to a boil. Add the pasta shells and cook for 10 minutes. Drain the shells, half fill the pot with cold water and place the shells in the water.

2 Melt the butter in a saucepan, add the onion and cook gently, stirring, for about 5 minutes, until softened. Add the spinach, garlic and saffron, then grate in plenty of nutmeg and add salt and pepper to taste. Stir well, increase the heat to medium and cook for 5–8 minutes, stirring frequently, until the spinach is wilted and tender.

3 Increase the heat to high and stir until the water boils off and the spinach is quite dry. Turn the spinach into a bowl, add the ricotta and beat well to mix. Taste for seasoning, then add the egg and beat well again.

4 Purée the tomato sauce in a blender or food processor, pour it into a measuring cup and fill it up to 3 cups with wine, stock or water. Add the cream, stir well to mix and taste for seasoning.

5 Spread about half the sauce over the bottom of six individual gratin dishes. Remove the pasta shells one at a time from the water, shake them well and fill them with the spinach and ricotta mixture, using a teaspoon. Arrange three shells in the center of each dish, spoon the remaining sauce over them, then cover with the grated Parmesan. Bake in the oven for 10–12 minutes or until hot. Allow to stand for about 5 minutes before serving.

Culurgiones
Sardinian Ravioli

THESE RAVIOLI, with their unusual mashed potato and mint filling, are from northern Sardinia. Here they are gratinéed in the oven with butter and cheese, but they are often served dressed with a tomato sauce.

INGREDIENTS

1 recipe Pasta with Eggs

1/4 cup butter

2/3 cup freshly grated pecorino cheese

For the filling

2 potatoes, each about 7 ounces, diced

generous 2/3 cup freshly grated hard salty pecorino cheese

3 ounces soft fresh pecorino cheese

1 egg yolk

1 generous handful fresh mint, leaves removed and chopped

good pinch of saffron powder

salt and ground black pepper

Serves 4–6

1 Make the filling. Cook the diced potatoes in salted boiling water for 15–20 minutes or until soft. Drain the potatoes and turn into a bowl, then mash until smooth. Set aside until cold. Add the cheeses, egg yolk, mint, saffron and salt and pepper to taste and stir well to mix.

2 Using a pasta machine, roll out one-quarter of the pasta into a 36-inch–40-inch strip. Cut the strip with a sharp knife into two 18–20-inch lengths.

3 With a fluted 4-inch biscuit cutter, cut out 4–5 circles from one of the pasta strips. Using a teaspoon, put a mound of filling on one side of each circle. Brush a little water around the edge of each circle, then fold the plain side of the circle over the filling to make a half-moon shape. Pleat the curved edge to seal.

4 Put the *culurgiones* on floured dish towels, sprinkle with flour and allow to dry. Repeat the process with the remaining dough to make 32–40 *culurgiones* altogether. If you have any stuffing left, re-roll the pasta trimmings and make more *culurgiones*.

5 Preheat the oven to 375°F. Cook the *culurgiones* in a large pot of salted boiling water for 4–5 minutes. Meanwhile, melt the butter in a small saucepan.

6 Drain the *culurgiones*, turn them into a large baking pan and pour the melted butter over them. Sprinkle with the grated pecorino and bake in the oven for 10–15 minutes, until golden and bubbly. Allow to stand for 5 minutes before serving.

COOK'S TIP

There is quite an art to pleating the curved edge of culurgiones, *but each cook has his or her own way of doing it, so don't worry about getting a precise finish. Do whatever you think looks best—some* culurgiones *look like miniature Cornish turnovers, others more like wontons. If you prefer, simply make square or round ravioli, or plain half-moons.*

Rotolo di Pasta Farcita

Stuffed Pasta Roll

THIS IS AN IMPRESSIVE dinner party first course. It takes quite a long time to make, but it can be made up to the baking stage the day before.

INGREDIENTS

6 tablespoons butter

1 small onion, finely chopped

5 ounces fresh spinach leaves, washed
  and trimmed

generous 1 cup ricotta cheese

1 egg

4 tablespoons freshly grated Parmesan cheese

4 tablespoons freshly grated pecorino cheese

nutmeg

$^2/_3$ recipe Pasta with Eggs

salt and ground black pepper

For the tomato sauce

4 tablespoons olive oil

1 onion, finely chopped

1 carrot, finely chopped

1 celery stalk, finely chopped

1 garlic clove, thinly sliced

a few leaves each fresh basil, thyme and
  oregano or marjoram, plus extra basil
  leaves, to garnish

2 cans (14-ounce) chopped Italian
  plum tomatoes

1 tablespoon sun-dried tomato paste

1 teaspoon sugar

5–7 tablespoons dry white wine

Serves 6

1 Melt 2 tablespoons of the butter in a medium saucepan, add the finely chopped onion and cook gently, stirring frequently, for about 5 minutes, until softened.

2 Add the spinach and salt and pepper to taste and cook over medium heat for 5–8 minutes, stirring frequently, until the spinach is wilted and tender. Increase the heat to high and stir until the water boils off and the spinach is quite dry.

3 Finely chop the spinach mixture in a food processor or by hand. Transfer to a bowl and add the ricotta, egg and half the grated Parmesan and pecorino. Season to taste with freshly grated nutmeg and salt, and add plenty of pepper. Beat well to mix.

4 Roll out the pasta dough to a 20 × 16-inch rectangle. Place the rectangle on a large piece of cheese-cloth with one of the short sides nearest you.

5 Spread the spinach mixture thinly over the pasta, leaving a $^3/_4$-inch margin along the two long sides and a 2-inch margin along the short side that is furthest away from you. Moisten the two long sides with water.

6 Starting from the short side that is nearest you, pick up the cloth and roll the pasta away from you as you would a jelly roll. Don't press it, just let it roll until you have a 16-inch long "sausage". Press the two open ends to seal the pasta, then roll the cloth around the *rotolo* a couple of times and tie the two ends tightly with string.

7 Half fill a fish steamer or large oval flameproof casserole with water and bring it to a boil. Add a large pinch of salt, then the *rotolo*. Half cover with a lid and simmer for 45 minutes, turning the *rotolo* over twice. Remove the *rotolo* from the water and place it on a board near the sink. Prop the board up at one end to allow the excess water to drain away from the *rotolo*, then set aside to cool.

8 Make the tomato sauce. Chop the onion, carrot and celery finely, either in a food processor or by hand. Heat the oil in a saucepan, add the garlic slices and stir over very low heat for 1–2 minutes. Add the chopped vegetables and the fresh herbs. Cook over low heat, stirring for 5–7 minutes, until the vegetables have softened and are lightly colored.

9 Add the tomatoes, tomato paste and sugar, then add salt and pepper to taste. Bring to a boil, stirring all the time, then lower the heat and simmer gently, uncovered, for about 45 minutes, stirring occasionally.

10 Preheat the oven to 400°F. Unwrap the *rotolo* and cut it into 12 thick slices. Melt the remaining butter and brush a little of it over the inside of six individual ovenproof dishes or a large shallow baking dish.

11 Arrange the *rotolo* slices slightly overlapping in the dishes or dish and drizzle the remaining butter over them. Sprinkle with the remaining Parmesan and pecorino and bake in the oven for 10–15 minutes or until golden brown.

12 Meanwhile, blend the tomato sauce in a food processor until smooth. Transfer the sauce to a pan and add enough wine to thin it down to a pouring consistency, then heat until bubbling. Serve the *rotolo* slices on individual plates, on a pool of tomato sauce, sprinkled with basil leaves.

COOK'S TIP

If you have a pasta machine, roll out half the dough into a 40-inch strip. Cut the strip with a sharp knife into two 20-inch lengths (you can do this during rolling if the strip gets too long to manage). Brush the long edge of one of the strips with water, then overlap the other strip on top by about 1/12-inch. Dust lightly with flour and press together, then seal the join by rolling over it with a rolling pin. Repeat with the remaining dough, then join the two pieces of pasta together in the same way so that you have a large rectangle.

Agnolotti di Taleggio e Maggiorama

Agnolotti with Taleggio and Marjoram

THE FILLING FOR THESE LITTLE half-moons is very simple—only two ingredients—but the combination of flavors is absolutely delicious.

INGREDIENTS

1 recipe Pasta with Eggs
12–14 ounces taleggio cheese
2 tablespoons finely chopped
    fresh marjoram, plus extra to garnish
1/2 cup butter
salt and ground black pepper
freshly grated Parmesan cheese, to serve

Serves 6–8

1 Using a pasta machine, roll out a quarter of the pasta into a 36-inch–40-inch strip. Cut the strip with a sharp knife into two 18–20-inch lengths (you can do this during rolling if the strip gets too long to manage).

2 Cut 8–10 little cubes of taleggio and place them along one side of one of the pasta strips, spacing them evenly. Sprinkle each taleggio cube with a little chopped marjoram and pepper to taste.

3 Brush a little water around each cube of cheese, then fold the plain side of the pasta strip over them.

4 Starting from the folded edge, press down gently with your fingertips around each cube, pushing the air out at the unfolded edge. Sprinkle lightly with flour.

5 Using only half of a 2-inch fluted round ravioli or biscuit cutter, cut around each cube of cheese to make a half-moon shape. The folded edge should be the straight edge.

6 If you like, press the cut edges of the agnolotti with the tines of a fork to give a decorative effect.

7 Put the agnolotti on floured dish towels, sprinkle lightly with flour and allow to dry while repeating the process with the remaining pasta, cheese, marjoram and pepper, to get 64–80 agnolotti altogether.

8 Drop the agnolotti into a large pot of salted boiling water, bring back to a boil and boil for 4–5 minutes until *al dente*.

9 Meanwhile, melt the butter in a small saucepan until it is sizzling.

10 Drain the agnolotti and divide them equally among six or eight warmed large bowls. Drizzle the sizzling butter over them and serve immediately, sprinkled with freshly grated Parmesan and chopped fresh marjoram. Hand around more grated Parmesan separately.

COOK'S TIPS

• *Taleggio is a square-shaped, semi-soft cheese from Lombardy. It is quite easy to get in large supermarkets, or any Italian delicatessen. It has a mild, slightly nutty flavor and good melting qualities. For this recipe, make sure that you remove the rind, which tends to be quite tough and salty.*
• *If you are unable to get taleggio, use fontina cheese instead, or a strongly flavored blue cheese, such as Gorgonzola. If you use a blue cheese, substitute sage for the marjoram.*

VARIATION

Marjoram is traditional with the taleggio cheese in this recipe, both for the filling and the sizzling butter, but you can use other fresh herbs, such as sage, basil or Italian parsley.

Pasticciata

Pasta Pie

THIS IS AN EXCELLENT SUPPER dish for vegetarians, and children absolutely love it. All the ingredients will probably already be in your pantry or refrigerator, so it makes a good "standby" meal if you have guests at short notice.

INGREDIENTS

2 tablespoons olive oil

1 small onion, finely chopped

1 can (14 ounces) chopped Italian plum tomatoes

1 tablespoon sun-dried tomato paste

1 teaspoon dried mixed herbs

1 teaspoon dried oregano or basil

1 teaspoon sugar

1 1/2 cups conchiglie or rigatoni

2 tablespoons freshly grated Parmesan cheese

2 tablespoons dried bread crumbs

salt and ground black pepper

For the white sauce

2 tablespoons butter

1/4 cup all-purpose flour

2 1/2 cups milk

1 egg

Serves 4

1 Heat the olive oil in a large skillet or saucepan and cook the finely chopped onion over gentle heat, stirring frequently, for about 5 minutes, until softened. Stir in the tomatoes. Fill the empty can with water and add it to the tomato mixture, with the tomato paste, herbs and sugar.

2 Add salt and pepper to taste and bring to a boil, stirring. Cover the pan, lower the heat and simmer, stirring occasionally, for 10–15 minutes.

3 Meanwhile, preheat the oven to 375°F. Cook the pasta according to the instructions on the package.

4 Meanwhile, make the white sauce. Melt the butter in a pan, add the flour and cook, stirring, for 1 minute.

5 Add the milk a little at a time, whisking well after each addition. Bring to a boil and cook, stirring, until the sauce is smooth and thick. Season, then remove the pan from heat.

6 Drain the pasta and turn it into a baking dish. Taste the tomato sauce and add salt and pepper. Pour the sauce into the dish and stir well to mix with the pasta.

7 Beat the egg into the white sauce, then pour the sauce over the pasta mixture. Separate the pasta with a fork in several places so that the white sauce fills the gaps.

8 Smooth the surface, sprinkle it with grated Parmesan and bread crumbs and bake for 15–20 minutes or until the topping is golden brown and the cheese is bubbling. Allow to stand for about 10 minutes before serving.

VARIATIONS

• *If you don't have any dried bread crumbs, you can cheat by crushing a package of chips and sprinkling them over the pasticciata instead. Children love this crisp topping, especially if you use their favorite flavor.*

• *You could add chunks of roasted vegetables, such as zucchini, bell peppers or eggplant to the tomato sauce if you like. This will add extra flavor and make a more substantial meal.*

• *For meat lovers, Bolognese sauce can be used instead of the tomato sauce.*

Lunch &Supper Dishes

Whether you are looking for an elaborate dinner party dish or for a quick lunch or supper, these recipes prove the enormous versatility of pasta. The fish and shellfish recipes create stunning and sophisticated dishes that taste fabulous and are perfect for impressing guests. Pasta dishes with cream sauces, such as *Elicoidali di Mezzanotte*, are unbelievably quick to make and are just right for famished revellers after a night out. When it comes to meat sauces, people tend to think of *Spaghetti alla Bolognese*, but this chapter introduces a regional favorite, which serves this popular sauce with cheese-stuffed cappellacci.

Most of the dishes in this chapter are easy to make but even making your own pasta can be easier than you think. A pasta machine can save a lot of time and effort, but much of the charm and fun of home-made pasta lies in its little imperfections.

Capelli d'Angelo all'Aragosta

Capelli d'Angelo with Lobster

THIS IS A SOPHISTICATED, stylish dish for a special occasion. Some cooks make the sauce with champagne rather than sparkling white wine, especially when they are planning to serve champagne with the meal.

INGREDIENTS

meat from the body, tail and claws of
   1 cooked lobster
juice of ¹/2 lemon
3 tablespoons butter
4 fresh tarragon sprigs, leaves stripped
   and chopped
4 tablespoons heavy cream
6 tablespoons sparkling dry white wine
4 tablespoons fish stock
11 ounces fresh capelli d'angelo
salt and ground black pepper
about 2 teaspoons sevruga caviar,
   to garnish (optional)

Serves 4

1 Cut the lobster meat into small pieces and put it in a bowl. Sprinkle with the lemon juice. Melt the butter in a skillet or large saucepan, add the lobster meat and tarragon and stir over the heat for a few seconds. Add the cream and stir for a few seconds more, then pour in the wine and stock, with salt and pepper to taste. Simmer for 2 minutes, then remove from heat and cover.

2 Cook the pasta according to the instructions on the package. Drain well, reserving a few spoonfuls of the cooking water.

3 Place the pan of lobster sauce over medium to high heat, add the pasta and toss for just long enough to combine and heat through; moisten with a little of the reserved water from the pasta. Serve immediately in warmed bowls, sprinkled with sevruga caviar if you like.

COOK'S TIP

To remove the meat from a lobster, place the lobster on a board with its underbelly facing uppermost. With a large sharp knife, cut the lobster in half lengthwise. Spoon out the green liver and any pink roe (coral) and reserve these, then remove and discard the gravel sac (stomach). Pull the white tail meat out from either side of the shell and discard the black intestinal vein. Crack the claws with a nutcracker just below the pincers and remove the meat from the base. Pull away the small pincer, taking the white membrane with it, then remove the meat from this part of the shell. Pull the meat from the large pincer shell.

Tagliolini con Vongole e Cozze

Tagliolini with Clams and Mussels

SERVED ON WHITE CHINA, this makes a stunning looking dish for a dinner party first course. The sauce can be prepared a few hours ahead of time, then the pasta cooked and the dish assembled at the last minute.

INGREDIENTS

I pound fresh mussels
I pound fresh hard-shell clams
4 tablespoons olive oil
I small onion, finely chopped
2 garlic cloves, finely chopped
I large handful fresh Italian parsley, plus
 extra chopped parsley to garnish
3/4 cup dry white wine
I cup fish stock
I small fresh red chile, seeded and chopped
I2 ounces squid ink tagliolini or tagliatelle
salt and ground black pepper
Serves 4

1 Scrub the mussels and clams under cold running water and discard any that are open or damaged, or that do not close when sharply tapped against the work surface.

2 Heat half the oil in a large pot, add the onion and cook gently for about 5 minutes until softened. Sprinkle in the garlic, then add about half the parsley sprigs, with salt and pepper to taste. Add the mussels and clams and pour in the wine. Cover with the lid and bring to a boil over a high heat. Cook for about 5 minutes, shaking the pan frequently, until the shellfish have opened.

3 Turn the mussels and clams into a fine strainer set over a bowl and let the liquid drain through. Discard the aromatics in the sieve, together with any mussels or clams that have failed to open. Return the liquid to the clean pot and add the fish stock. Chop the remaining parsley finely and add it to the liquid with the chopped chile. Bring to a boil, then lower the heat and simmer, stirring, for a few minutes until slightly reduced. Turn off the heat.

4 Remove and discard the top shells from about half the mussels and clams. Put all the mussels and clams in the pan of liquid and seasonings, then cover the pan tightly and set aside.

5 Cook the pasta according to the instructions on the package.

6 Drain well, then return to the clean pot; toss with the remaining olive oil. Put the pot of shellfish over a high heat and toss to quickly heat the shellfish through and combine with the liquid and seasonings.

7 Divide the pasta among four warmed plates, spoon the shellfish mixture over and around, then serve immediately, sprinkled with parsley.

Cappellacci alla Bolognese

Cheese Cappellacci with Bolognese Sauce

IN EMILIA-ROMAGNA it is traditional to serve these *cappellacci* with a rich meat sauce, but if you prefer you can serve them with a tomato sauce, or just melted butter.

INGREDIENTS

1 recipe Pasta with Eggs
8 cups beef stock made with stock cubes and water or diluted canned consommé
freshly grated Parmesan cheese, to serve
basil leaves, to garnish

For the filling

generous 1 cup ricotta cheese
3 1/2 ounces taleggio cheese, rind removed, diced very small
4 tablespoons freshly grated Parmesan cheese
1 small egg
nutmeg
salt and ground black pepper

For the Bolognese meat sauce

2 tablespoons butter
1 tablespoon olive oil
1 onion
2 carrots
2 celery stalks
2 garlic cloves
4 1/2 ounces pancetta or lean bacon, diced
9 ounces lean ground beef
9 ounces lean ground pork
1/2 cup dry white wine
2 cans (14-ounce) crushed Italian plum tomatoes
2–3 cups beef stock
scant 1/2 cup panna da cucina or heavy cream

Serves 6

1 Make the filling. Put the ricotta, taleggio and grated Parmesan in a bowl and mash together with a fork.

2 Add the egg and freshly grated nutmeg and salt and pepper to taste and stir well to mix.

3 Using a pasta machine, roll out one-quarter of the pasta into a 36-inch–40-inch strip. Cut the strip with a sharp knife into two 18–20-inch lengths (you can do this during rolling if the strip gets too long to manage).

4 Using a 2 1/2–3-inch square ravioli cutter, cut 6–7 squares from one of the pasta strips. Using a teaspoon, put a mound of filling in the center of each square. Brush a little water around the edge of each square, then fold the square diagonally in half over the filling to make a triangular shape. Press to seal.

5 Wrap the triangle around one of your index fingers, bringing the bottom two corners together. Pinch the ends together to seal, then press with your fingertip around the top edge of the filling to make an indentation so that the "hat" looks like a bishop's miter.

6 Place the *cappellacci* on floured dish towels, sprinkle them lightly with flour and allow to dry while repeating the process with the remaining dough, to make 48–56 *cappellacci* altogether.

7 Make the meat sauce. Heat the butter and oil in a large skillet or saucepan until sizzling. Add the vegetables, garlic, and the pancetta or bacon and cook over medium heat, stirring frequently, for 10 minutes or until the vegetables have softened.

8 Add the ground beef and pork, lower the heat and cook gently for 10 minutes, stirring frequently and breaking up any lumps in the meat with a wooden spoon. Stir in salt and pepper to taste, then add the wine and stir again. Simmer for about 5 minutes, or until reduced.

9 Add the tomatoes and 1 cup of the stock and bring to a boil. Stir well, then lower the heat, half cover the pan with a lid and allow to simmer very gently for 2 hours. Stir occasionally during this time and add more stock as it becomes absorbed.

10 Add the *panna da cucina* or heavy cream to the meat sauce. Stir well to mix, then simmer the sauce, without a lid, for another 30 minutes, stirring frequently.

11 Bring the stock to a boil in a large saucepan.

12 Drop the *cappellacci* into the stock, bring back to a boil and boil for 4–5 minutes; drain the *cappellacci* and divide them equally among six warmed bowls. Spoon the hot Bolognese sauce over the *cappellacci* and sprinkle with grated Parmesan and basil leaves. Serve immediately.

COOK'S TIP

The exact shape of cappellacci *varies from one cook to another. Some are made from circles rather than squares of pasta, although these are more often called* tortellini *or* tortelloni. *It all depends on the region in which they are made. If you prefer a party-hat shape to a bishop's miter, don't make an indentation above the filling in Step 5, but instead turn up the bottom edge of each "hat" so that they have brims.* Cappelletti *are the same shape as* cappellacci *but are made from smaller squares of pasta (about 2-inches square). Not surprisingly, because of their size,* cappelletti *are trickier to make.*

Ravioli con la Zucca

Ravioli with Pumpkin

THIS IS A VERY SIMPLE VERSION of a Christmas Eve specialty from Lombardy. In traditional recipes the pumpkin filling is flavored with *mostarda di frutta* (a kind of sweet fruit pickle), crushed amaretti biscuits and sugar. Here the pumpkin is seasoned with Parmesan and nutmeg. It is quite sweet enough for most tastes.

INGREDIENTS

1 recipe Pasta with Eggs
¹/2 cup butter
freshly grated Parmesan cheese, to serve

For the filling
1 pound piece of pumpkin
1 tablespoon olive oil
scant ¹/4 cup freshly grated Parmesan cheese
nutmeg
salt and ground black pepper
Serves 8

1 Make the filling. Preheat the oven to 425°F. Cut the piece of pumpkin into chunks and remove the seeds and fibers. Put the chunks, skin side down, in a roasting pan and drizzle the oil over the pumpkin flesh. Roast in the oven for 30 minutes, turning the pieces over once or twice.

2 Set aside the roasted pumpkin until it is cool enough to handle, then scrape the flesh out into a bowl and discard the pumpkin skin.

3 Mash the roasted pumpkin flesh with a fork, then add the grated Parmesan and freshly grated nutmeg and salt and pepper to taste. Stir well to mix, then set aside until cold.

4 Using a pasta machine, roll out one-quarter of the pasta into a 36-inch–40-inch strip. Cut the strip with a sharp knife into two 18–20-inch lengths (you can do this during rolling if the strip gets too long to manage).

5 Using a teaspoon, put 10–12 little mounds of the filling along one side of one of the pasta strips, spacing them evenly.

6 Brush a little water around each mound, then fold the plain side of the pasta strip over the mounds of filling. Starting from the folded edge, press down gently with your fingertips around each mound, pushing the air out at the unfolded edge. Sprinkle lightly with flour.

7 With a fluted pasta wheel, cut along each long side, then in between each mound to make small square shapes. Put the ravioli on floured dish towels, sprinkle lightly with flour and allow to dry, while repeating the process with the remaining pasta, to get 80–96 ravioli altogether.

8 Drop the ravioli into a large pot of salted boiling water, bring back to a boil and boil for 4–5 minutes. Meanwhile, melt the butter in a small saucepan until it is sizzling.

9 Drain the ravioli and divide them equally among eight warmed dinner plates or large bowls. Drizzle the sizzling butter over the ravioli and serve immediately, sprinkled with grated Parmesan. Pass more grated Parmesan separately.

VARIATION

You can buy mostarda di frutta *at Italian markets, especially at Christmas time. If you would like to try some in the filling, add about 3 tablespoons, together with a few crushed amaretti.*

Ravioli alla Romagnola

Ravioli with Pork and Turkey

THIS ROMAN-STYLE RAVIOLI stuffed with ground meat and cheese is scented with fresh herbs. It makes a substantial first course.

INGREDIENTS

1 recipe Pasta with Eggs

¼ cup butter

a large bunch of fresh sage, leaves removed and coarsely chopped

4 tablespoons freshly grated Parmesan cheese

extra sage leaves and freshly grated Parmesan cheese, to serve

For the filling

2 tablespoons butter

5 ounces ground pork

4 ounces ground turkey

4 fresh sage leaves, finely chopped

1 sprig of fresh rosemary, leaves removed and finely chopped

2 tablespoons dry white wine

generous ¼ cup ricotta cheese

3 tablespoons freshly grated Parmesan cheese

1 egg

nutmeg

salt and ground black pepper

Serves 8

1 Make the filling. Melt the butter in a medium saucepan, add the ground pork and turkey and the herbs and cook gently for 5–6 minutes, stirring frequently and breaking up any lumps in the meat with a wooden spoon. Add salt and pepper to taste and stir to mix.

2 Add the wine to the pan and stir again. Simmer for 1–2 minutes, until reduced slightly, then cover the pan and simmer gently for about 20 minutes, stirring occasionally. With a slotted spoon, transfer the meat to a bowl and set aside to cool.

3 Add the ricotta and Parmesan cheeses to the bowl with the egg and freshly grated nutmeg to taste. Stir well to mix the ingredients thoroughly.

4 Using a pasta machine, roll out one-quarter of the pasta into a 36-inch–40-inch strip. Cut the strip with a sharp knife into two 18–20-inch lengths (you can do this during rolling if the strip gets too long to manage).

5 Using a teaspoon, put 10–12 little mounds of the filling along one side of one of the pasta strips, spacing them evenly. Brush a little water onto the pasta strip around each mound, then fold the plain side of the pasta strip over the filling.

6 Starting from the folded edge, press down gently with your fingertips around each mound of filling, pushing the air out at the unfolded edge. Sprinkle lightly with flour.

7 With a fluted pasta wheel, cut along each long side, then in between each mound to make small square shapes. Dust lightly with flour.

8 Put the ravioli in a single layer on floured dish towels and set aside to dry while repeating the process with the remaining pasta, to make 80–96 ravioli altogether.

9 Drop the ravioli into a large pot of salted boiling water, bring back to a boil and boil for 4–5 minutes.

COOK'S TIP

Ground pork and turkey are widely available at supermarkets, but if you cannot get one or the other you can use just one type of meat, or substitute ground veal, beef or lamb to use in the ravioli filling.

10 While the ravioli are cooking, melt the butter in a small saucepan, add the fresh sage leaves and stir over medium to high heat until the sage leaves are sizzling in the butter.

11 Drain the ravioli and pour half into a warmed large bowl. Sprinkle with half the grated Parmesan, then half the sage butter. Repeat with the remaining ravioli, Parmesan and sage butter. Serve immediately, garnished with fresh sage leaves. Pass more grated Parmesan separately.

Spaghetti alla Carbonara

Spaghetti with Eggs, Bacon and Cream

AN ALL-TIME FAVORITE that needs no introducing. This version has plenty of pancetta or bacon and is not too creamy, but you can vary the amounts as you please.

INGREDIENTS

2 tablespoons olive oil

1 small onion, finely chopped

8 pancetta or lean bacon strips, cut into
   1/2-inch strips

12 ounces fresh or dried spaghetti

4 eggs

4 tablespoons crème fraîche

4 tablespoons freshly grated Parmesan
   cheese, plus extra to serve

salt and ground black pepper

Serves 4

1 Heat the oil in a large saucepan or skillet, add the finely chopped onion and cook over low heat, stirring frequently, for about 5 minutes until softened but not colored.

2 Add the strips of pancetta or bacon to the onion in the pan and cook for about 10 minutes, stirring almost all the time. Meanwhile, cook the pasta in a pot of salted boiling water according to the instructions on the package until *al dente*.

3 Put the eggs, crème fraîche and grated Parmesan in a bowl. Grind in plenty of pepper, then beat everything together well.

4 Drain the pasta, turn it into the pan with the pancetta or bacon and toss well to mix. Turn the heat off under the pan. Immediately add the egg mixture and toss vigorously so that it cooks lightly and coats the pasta.

5 Quickly taste for seasoning, then divide among four warmed bowls and sprinkle with black pepper. Serve immediately, with extra grated Parmesan passed separately.

Elicoidali di Mezzanotte

Elicoidali with Cheese and Cream

MEZZANOTE MEANS MIDDLE of the night, which is when this rich and filling dish is traditionally eaten after a night out. It is very quick, so if you have a carton of ricotta in the refrigerator it also makes a simple evening meal.

INGREDIENTS

3¹/₂ cups elicoidali

3 egg yolks

7 tablespoons freshly grated Parmesan cheese

scant 1 cup ricotta cheese

4 tablespoons panna da cucina or heavy cream

nutmeg

3 tablespoons butter

salt and ground black pepper

Serves 4

1 Cook the pasta according to the instructions on the package.

2 Meanwhile, mix the egg yolks, grated Parmesan and ricotta together in a bowl. Add the cream and mix with a fork.

3 Grate in nutmeg to taste, then season with plenty of black pepper and a little salt. Drain the pasta thoroughly when cooked. Return the clean pot to the heat. Melt the butter, add the drained pasta and toss vigorously over medium heat.

4 Turn off the heat under the pot and add the ricotta mixture. Stir well with a large spoon for 10–15 seconds until all the pasta is coated in sauce. Serve immediately, in warmed individual bowls.

COOK'S TIP

Elicoidali are a short tubular pasta with curved ridges. If you can't get them, use rigatoni, which have straight ridges.

Baked Pasta Dishes

Like Bolognese sauce, lasagne, macaroni cheese and cannelloni have become so popular outside Italy that we seldom stop to consider the origins of these delicious pasta dishes. A kind of layered pasta pie was mentioned by the Roman gastronome Apicius in the first century AD, so we know that lasagne, at least, has a very long history. In the Renaissance, sumptuous layered pasta dishes were popular with the wealthy.

Nowadays, *pasta al forno*, as baked pasta dishes are called in Italy, are more often eaten at family meals, especially on occasions when large numbers must be catered for. Baked dishes can be prepared in advance and are easy to serve. This chapter features classic dishes, such as *Lasagne Bolognesi,* and regional favorites with modern adaptations, such as *Cannelloni alla Sorrentina.*

Maccheroni ai Quattro Formaggi

Macaroni with Four Cheeses

RICH AND CREAMY, this is a deluxe macaroni and cheese casserole that can be served for an informal lunch or supper party. It goes well with both a tomato and basil salad or a leafy green salad.

INGREDIENTS

2¼ cups short-cut macaroni
¼ cup butter
½ cup all-purpose flour
2½ cups milk
scant ½ cup *panna da cucina* or
　heavy cream
scant ½ cup dry white wine
½ cup grated *Gruyère* or *Emmental* cheese
2 ounces fontina cheese, diced small
2 ounces Gorgonzola cheese, crumbled
1 cup freshly grated Parmesan cheese
salt and ground black pepper

Serves 4

3 Add the Gruyère or Emmental, fontina and Gorgonzola and about a third of the grated Parmesan to the sauce. Stir well to mix in the cheeses, then taste for seasoning and add salt and pepper if necessary.

4 Drain the pasta well and turn it into a baking pan. Pour the sauce over the pasta and mix well, then sprinkle the remaining Parmesan over the top. Bake for 25–30 minutes or until golden brown. Serve hot.

1 Preheat the oven to 350°F. Cook the pasta according to the instructions on the package.

2 Meanwhile, gently melt the butter in a medium saucepan, add the flour and cook, stirring, for 1–2 minutes. Add the milk a little at a time, whisking vigorously after each addition. Stir in the cream, followed by the dry white wine. Bring to a boil. Cook, stirring constantly until the sauce thickens, then remove the sauce from heat.

Lasagne Bolognesi

Lasagne from Bologna

THIS IS THE CLASSIC *lasagne al forno*. It is based on a rich, meaty filling, as you would expect from an authentic Bolognese recipe.

INGREDIENTS

1 recipe Bolognese Meat Sauce
2/3–1 cup hot beef stock, or water with stock cube
12 precooked dried lasagne sheets
2/3 cup freshly grated Parmesan cheese

For the white sauce
1/4 cup butter
1/2 cup all-purpose flour
3 3/4 cups hot milk
salt and ground black pepper

Serves 6

1 Preheat the oven to 375°F. If the Bolognese sauce is cold, reheat it. Once it is hot, stir in enough stock to make it quite runny.

2 Make the white sauce. Melt the butter in a medium saucepan, add the flour and cook, stirring, for 1–2 minutes. Add the milk a little at a time, whisking vigorously after each addition. Bring to a boil and cook, stirring, until the sauce is smooth and thick. Add salt and pepper to taste, whisk well to mix, then remove from heat.

3 Spread about a third of the Bolognese sauce over the bottom of a baking pan.

4 Cover the Bolognese sauce in the bottom of the dish with about a quarter of the white sauce, followed by four sheets of lasagne. Repeat the layers twice more, then cover the top layer of lasagne with the remaining white sauce and sprinkle the grated Parmesan evenly over the top.

5 Bake for 40–45 minutes or until the pasta feels tender when pierced with a skewer. Allow to stand for about 10 minutes before serving.

COOK'S TIPS

• The Bolognese sauce can be made up to 3 days in advance and kept in a covered container in the refrigerator.
• The lasagne is best baked immediately after layering or the pasta will begin to absorb the sauces and dry out.
• To reheat leftover lasagne, prick it all over with a skewer, then slowly pour a little milk over to moisten. Cover with foil and reheat in a 375°F oven for 20 minutes, or until bubbling.

Cannelloni con Ripieno di Carne

Cannelloni Stuffed with Meat

THIS IS A RICH AND SUBSTANTIAL dish, which takes quite a long time to prepare. Serve it for a party—it can be made a day ahead up to the baking stage. Your guests are bound to appreciate your efforts, because the cannelloni taste so good.

INGREDIENTS

1 tablespoon olive oil
1 small onion, finely chopped
1 pound ground beef
1 garlic clove, finely chopped
1 teaspoon dried mixed herbs
1/2 cup beef stock
1 egg
3 ounces cooked ham or mortadella
    sausage, finely chopped
3 tablespoons fine fresh white
    bread crumbs
1 2/3 cups freshly grated Parmesan cheese
18 precooked cannelloni tubes
salt and ground black pepper

For the tomato sauce
2 tablespoons olive oil
1 small onion, finely chopped
1/2 carrot, finely chopped
1 celery stalk, finely chopped
1 garlic clove, crushed
1 can (14 ounces) chopped Italian
    plum tomatoes
a few sprigs of fresh basil
1/2 teaspoon dried oregano

For the white sauce
1/4 cup butter
1/2 cup all-purpose flour
3 3/4 cups milk
nutmeg
Serves 6

1 Heat the olive oil in a medium skillet or saucepan and cook the finely chopped onion over gentle heat, stirring occasionally, for about 5 minutes, until softened.

2 Add the ground beef and garlic and cook gently for 10 minutes, stirring and breaking up any lumps with a wooden spoon. Add the mixed herbs, and salt and pepper to taste, then moisten with half the stock. Cover the pan and simmer for 25 minutes, stirring from time to time and adding more stock as the mixture reduces. Spoon into a bowl and allow to cool.

3 Meanwhile, make the tomato sauce. Heat the olive oil in a medium saucepan, add the vegetables and garlic and cook over medium heat, stirring frequently, for about 10 minutes. Add the canned tomatoes. Fill the empty can with water, pour it into the pan, then stir in the herbs, with salt and pepper to taste. Bring to a boil, lower the heat, cover and simmer for 25–30 minutes, stirring occasionally. Purée the tomato sauce in a blender or food processor.

4 Add the egg, ham or mortadella, bread crumbs and 6 tablespoons of the grated Parmesan to the meat and stir well to mix. Taste for seasoning.

5 Spread a little of the tomato sauce over the bottom of a baking pan. Using a teaspoon, fill the cannelloni tubes with the meat mixture and place them in a single layer in the dish on top of the tomato sauce. Pour the remaining tomato sauce over the top.

6 Preheat the oven to 375°F. Make the white sauce. Melt the butter in a saucepan, add the flour and cook, stirring, for 1–2 minutes. Add the milk a little at a time, whisking vigorously after each addition.

7 Bring to a boil and cook, stirring, until the sauce is smooth and thick. Grate in fresh nutmeg to taste and season with a little salt and pepper. Whisk well, then remove from heat.

8 Pour the white sauce over the stuffed cannelloni, then sprinkle with the remaining Parmesan. Place in the oven and bake for 40–45 minutes or until the cannelloni tubes feel tender when pierced with a skewer. Allow the cannelloni to stand for about 10 minutes before serving.

Pasticcio di Fusilli
Fusilli with Ham and Cheese

WITH ITS CRISPY CRUST and moist and creamy center, this quick and easy pasta casserole is both filling and nutritious. Serve it for a winter supper, with a salad on the side.

INGREDIENTS

2¾ cups fusilli, eliche or other
    short pasta shapes
3 eggs
scant 1 cup milk
²⁄₃ cup light cream
5 ounces Gruyère cheese, grated
nutmeg
4 ounces cooked ham, cut into strips
2 tablespoons freshly grated
    Parmesan cheese
salt and ground black pepper
Serves 4

1 Preheat the oven to 375°F. Bring a large pot of salted water to a boil. Add the pasta and cook for 5 minutes.

2 Meanwhile, beat the eggs in a cup with the milk, cream and half the grated Gruyère. Grate in a little fresh nutmeg and season to taste.

3 Drain the pasta and turn half of it into a buttered baking pan. Arrange half the strips of ham on top, then follow with the remaining pasta and ham. Pour the egg and cream mixture into the pan, stir to mix a little, then sprinkle the remaining Gruyère and the Parmesan over the top. Bake for 30 minutes or until golden brown.

Lasagne al Ragù d'Agnello
Lasagne with Lamb

IT IS UNUSUAL TO MAKE lasagne with lamb, but the flavor is excellent.

INGREDIENTS

1 tablespoon olive oil
1 small onion, finely chopped
1 pound ground lamb
1 garlic clove, crushed
3 tablespoons dry white wine
1 teaspoon dried mixed herbs
1 teaspoon dried oregano
scant 2 cups tomato sauce
12–16 fresh lasagne sheets, precooked
    if necessary
2 tablespoons freshly grated Parmesan cheese
salt and ground black pepper

For the white sauce
½ cup butter
½ cup all-purpose flour
3¾ cups hot milk
2 tablespoons freshly grated Parmesan cheese
nutmeg
Serves 4–6

1 Heat the oil in a saucepan and cook the onion over gentle heat, stirring frequently, for about 5 minutes, until softened. Add the ground lamb and garlic and cook gently for 10 minutes, stirring frequently. Stir in salt and pepper to taste, then add the wine and cook rapidly for about 2 minutes, stirring constantly. Stir in the herbs and tomato sauce. Simmer gently for 45 minutes to 1 hour, stirring occasionally.

2 Preheat the oven to 375°F. Make the white sauce. Melt the butter in a saucepan, add the flour and cook, stirring, for 1–2 minutes. Add the milk a little at a time, whisking vigorously after each addition. Bring to a boil and cook, stirring, until the sauce is smooth and thick. Add the Parmesan, grate in fresh nutmeg to taste, season with a little salt and pepper and whisk well. Remove the pan from heat.

3 Spread a few spoonfuls of meat sauce over the bottom of a baking pan and cover with three or four sheets of lasagne. Spread a quarter of the remaining meat sauce over the lasagne, then quarter of the white sauce. Repeat the layers three times, finishing with white sauce.

4 Sprinkle the Parmesan over the surface and bake for 30–40 minutes or until the topping is golden brown and bubbling. Allow to stand for about 10 minutes before serving.

Lasagne ai Funghi e Zucchine

Mushroom and Zucchini Lasagne

THIS IS THE PERFECT main-course lasagne for vegetarians. Adding dried porcini to fresh cremini mushrooms intensifies the "mushroomy" flavor and gives the whole dish more substance. Serve with crusty Italian bread.

INGREDIENTS

$^{1}/_{2}$ ounce dried porcini mushrooms

$^{3}/_{4}$ cup warm water

2 tablespoons olive oil

6 tablespoons butter

1 pound zucchini, thinly sliced

1 onion, finely chopped

6 cups (about 1 pound) cremini
  mushrooms, thinly sliced

2 garlic cloves, crushed

1 recipe Winter Tomato Sauce

2 teaspoons chopped fresh marjoram or
  1 teaspoon dried marjoram, plus extra
  fresh leaves, to garnish

6–8 precooked lasagne sheets

$^{2}/_{3}$ cup freshly grated
  Parmesan cheese

salt and ground black pepper

For the white sauce

3 tablespoons butter

$^{1}/_{3}$ cup all-purpose flour

$3^{3}/_{4}$ cups hot milk

nutmeg

Serves 6

1 Put the dried porcini mushrooms in a bowl. Pour over the warm water and allow to soak for 15–20 minutes. Turn the porcini and liquid into a fine sieve set over a bowl and squeeze the mushrooms with your hands to release as much liquid as possible. Chop the mushrooms finely and set aside. Strain the soaking liquid through a fine sieve and reserve half for the sauce.

2 Preheat the oven to 375°F. Heat the olive oil with 2 tablespoons of the butter in a large skillet or saucepan.

3 Add about half the zucchini slices to the pan and season with salt and pepper to taste. Cook the zucchini over medium heat, turning the slices frequently, for 5–8 minutes until they are lightly colored on both sides. Remove the zucchini from the pan with a slotted spoon and allow to drain on paper towels. Repeat with the remaining zucchini.

4 Melt half the remaining butter in the fat remaining in the pan, then cook the finely chopped onion, stirring, for 1–2 minutes. Add half of the fresh mushrooms and the crushed garlic to the pan and sprinkle with a little salt and pepper to taste.

5 Toss the mushrooms over high heat for 5 minutes or so, until the mushrooms are juicy and tender. Transfer to a bowl with a slotted spoon, then repeat with the remaining butter and mushrooms.

6 Make the white sauce. Melt the butter in a large saucepan, add the flour and cook, stirring, over medium heat for 1–2 minutes.

7 Acd the hot milk a little at a time, whisking well after each addition. Bring tc a boil and cook, stirring, until the sauce is smooth and thick. Grate in fresh nutmeg to taste and season with a little salt and pepper. Whisk well, then remove the sauce from heat.

8 Place the tomato sauce in a blender or food processor with the reserved porcini soaking liquid and blend to a pureé. Add the zucchini to the bowl of fried mushrooms, then stir in the porcini and marjoram.

9 Adjust the seasoning to taste, then spread a third of the tomato sauce in a baking pan. Add half the vegetable mixture, spreading it evenly.

10 Top with about a third of the white sauce, then about half the lasagne sheets. Repeat these layers, then top with the remaining tomato sauce and white sauce and sprinkle with the grated Parmesan cheese.

11 Bake the lasagne for 35–40 minutes, or until the pasta feels tender when pierced with a skewer. Allow to stand for about 10 minutes before serving. If you like, sprinkle each serving with marjoram leaves.

COOK'S TIPS

• *The amount of pasta will depend on the size and shape of the pasta sheets and your baking dish; you may need to break the pasta to fit.*

• *This dish is time-consuming to prepare, but well worth the effort. You can make the tomato sauce in advance and chill it for up to 2 days, until you are ready to assemble the lasagne, or you can freeze it. Make sure that you allow it to thaw completely before using.*

Spaghetti Tetrazzini

Spaghetti and Turkey in Cheese Sauce

AN ITALIAN-AMERICAN RECIPE, Spaghetti Tetrazzini makes an excellent family meal. It is quite filling and rich, so serve it with a tossed green salad.

INGREDIENTS

6 tablespoons butter

12 ounces turkey breast fillet, cut into thin strips

2 pieces bottled roasted pepper, drained, rinsed, dried and cut into thin strips

6 ounces spaghetti

1/2 cup all-purpose flour

3 3/4 cups hot milk

1 1/3 cups freshly grated Parmesan cheese

1/4–1/2 teaspoon mustard powder

salt and ground black pepper

Serves 4–6

1 Melt about a third of the butter in a saucepan, add the turkey and sprinkle with a little salt and plenty of pepper. Toss the turkey over medium heat for about 5 minutes, until the meat turns white, then add the roasted pepper strips and toss to mix. Remove with a slotted spoon and set aside.

2 Preheat the oven to 350°F. Cook the pasta according to the instructions on the package.

3 Meanwhile, melt the remaining butter over low heat in the pan in which the turkey was cooked. Sprinkle in the flour and cook, stirring, for 1–2 minutes, then increase the heat to medium.

4 Add the hot milk a little at a time, whisking vigorously after each addition. Bring to a boil and cook, stirring, until the sauce is smooth and thick. Add two thirds of the grated Parmesan, then whisk in mustard, salt and pepper to taste. Remove the sauce from heat.

5 Drain the pasta and return it to the clean pot. Mix in half the cheese sauce, then spoon the mixture around the edge of a baking dish. Stir the turkey mixture into the remaining cheese sauce and spoon into the center of the dish. Sprinkle the remaining Parmesan evenly over the tetrazzini and bake for 15–20 minutes, until the cheese topping is just crisp. Serve hot.

Lasagne di Mare

Shellfish Lasagne

THIS IS A LUXURY LASAGNE suitable for an informal supper or lunch party. It is quite expensive to make, but the flavor is superb, so put it on your list for special occasion meals.

INGREDIENTS

4–6 fresh sea scallops

1 pound peeled raw large shrimp

1 garlic clove, crushed

6 tablespoons butter

1/2 cup all-purpose flour

2 1/2 cups hot milk

scant 1/2 cup panna da cucina or heavy cream

1/2 cup dry white wine

2 envelopes saffron powder

good pinch of cayenne pepper

4 1/2 ounces fontina cheese, thinly sliced

1 cup freshly grated Parmesan cheese

6–8 fresh egg lasagne sheets

salt and ground black pepper

Serves 4–6

1 Preheat the oven to 375°F. Cut the scallops and shrimp into bite-size pieces and spread out in a dish. Sprinkle with the garlic and salt and pepper to taste. Melt about a third of the butter in a medium saucepan, add the scallops and shrimp and toss over medium heat for 1–2 minutes or just until the shrimp turn pink. Remove the shellfish with a slotted spoon and set aside.

2 Add the remaining butter to the pan and melt over low heat. Sprinkle in the flour and cook, stirring, for 1–2 minutes, then increase the heat to medium and add the hot milk a little at a time, whisking vigorously after each addition. Bring to a boil and cook, stirring, until the sauce is smooth and very thick. Whisk in the cream, wine, saffron powder, cayenne and salt and pepper to taste, then remove the sauce from heat.

3 Spread about a third of the sauce over the bottom of a baking dish. Arrange half the fontina slices over the sauce and sprinkle with about a third of the grated Parmesan. Scatter about half the shellfish evenly on top, then cover with half the lasagne sheets. Repeat the layers, then cover with the remaining sauce and Parmesan.

4 Bake the lasagne for 30–40 minutes or until the topping is golden brown and bubbling. Let stand for 10 minutes before serving.

Cannelloni alla Sorrentina

Cannelloni Sorrentina-style

THERE'S MORE THAN ONE way of making cannelloni. For this fresh-tasting dish, sheets of cooked lasagne are rolled around a tomato filling to make a delicious main course for a summer dinner party. The ingredients are similar to those used on a Neapolitan pizza.

INGREDIENTS

4 tablespoons olive oil
I small onion, finely chopped
2 pounds ripe Italian plum tomatoes,
   peeled and finely chopped
2 garlic cloves, crushed
I large handful fresh basil leaves, shredded,
   plus extra basil leaves, to garnish
I cup vegetable stock
I cup dry white wine
2 tablespoons sun-dried tomato paste
1/2 teaspoon sugar
16–18 fresh or dried lasagne sheets
generous I cup ricotta cheese
4 1/2 ounces fresh mozzarella cheese,
   drained and diced small
8 bottled anchovy fillets in olive oil, drained
   and halved lengthwise
2/3 cup freshly grated Parmesan cheese
salt and ground black pepper
Serves 4–6

I Heat the oil in a medium saucepan, add the onion and cook gently, stirring frequently, for about 5 minutes, until softened. Stir in the tomatoes, garlic and half the basil. Season with salt and pepper to taste and toss over medium to high heat for 5 minutes.

2 Scoop about half the tomato mixture out of the pan, place in a bowl and set it aside to cool.

3 Stir the vegetable stock, white wine, tomato paste and sugar into the tomato mixture remaining in the pan and simmer for about 20 minutes, stirring occasionally.

4 Meanwhile, cook the lasagne sheets in batches in a saucepan of salted boiling water, according to the instructions on the package. Drain and separate the sheets of lasagne and lay them out flat on a clean dish towel.

VARIATION

For vegetarians, use 8 pitted black olives instead of the anchovies. Chop them coarsely and sprinkle them in a line along the length of the cannelloni filling.

5 Preheat the oven to 375°F. Add the ricotta and mozzarella to the tomato mixture in the bowl. Stir in the remaining basil and season to taste with salt and pepper.

6 Spread a little of the mixture over each lasagne sheet. Place an anchovy fillet across the width of each sheet, close to one of the short ends. Starting from the end with the anchovy, roll each lasagne sheet up like a Swiss roll.

7 Purée the tomato sauce in a blender or food processor. Spread a little of the tomato sauce over the bottom of a large baking pan. Arrange the cannelloni seam-side down in a single layer in the dish and spoon the remaining sauce over them.

8 Sprinkle the Parmesan over the top and bake for 20 minutes or until the topping is golden brown and bubbling. Serve hot, garnished with basil leaves.

acciughe see anchovies
aceto, 57
    see also balsamic vinegar
acini de pepe, 23
aglio see garlic
agnolotti, 22, 29, 49
    meat-filled with vodka
        sauce, 70–1
    with Taleggio and
        marjoram, 96
agnolotti: alla salsa di
        vodka, 70–1
    di Taleggio e
        maggiorama, 96
al dente, 9, 38
alfabeti and alfabetini, 23
alloro, 54
amounts of pasta to
        serve, 11, 38
anchovies, 58
anellini, 23
arlecchino, 25
arrabbiata sauce,
        commercial, 63
arugula, 55
    orecchiette with, 89

bacon: spaghetti with eggs,
        bacon and cream, 110
    see also ham; pancetta
ballerine, 25
balsamic vinegar, 57
    fusilli with tomato and
        balsamic vinegar
        sauce, 84
banane, 25

basil, 54
    see also pesto
basilico, 54
bavette, 12, 25
bay, 54
beef: Bolognese sauce with
        red wine, 72
    cannelloni stuffed with
        meat, 116
    cheese cappellacci with
        Bolognese sauce, 104–5

bell peppers, 60
benfatti, 16
black pepper, 56
    flavored pasta, 51
Bolognese sauce with red
        wine, 72
bottarga, 58–9
bow-ties see farfalle
brodo, 22
bucatini, 13

cannella, 56
cannelloni, 22, 30, 44, 47
    Sorrentina-style, 124
    stuffed with meat, 116
cannelloni: alla
        sorrentina, 124
    con ripieno di carne, 116
capel venere, 13
capelli d'angelo, 13, 27
    with lobster, 102
capelli d'angelo
        all'aragosta, 102
capers, 57
cappellacci, 30, 50
    cheese cappellacci
        with Bolognese
        sauce, 104–5
cappellacci alla
        bolognese, 104–5
cappelletti, 22, 29, 50
capperi see capers
capricciosa all'uovo, 12
caramelle, 31
carbonara sauce,
        commercial, 63
carrots: three-color
        tagliatelle, 82
caserecce, 19
cheeses, 62–3
    cheese cappellacci
        with Bolognese
        sauce, 104–5
    macaroni with four, 114
    see also individual types
        e.g. Parmesan
chicken: penne with
        chicken, broccoli and
        cheese, 75
chifferini, 16
chiles, 56
    flavored pasta, 51
chioccioloni, 22, 25
chitarra, 13, 47
cinnamon, 56
clams, 59
    tagliolini with clams
        and mussels, 103

vermicelli with clam
        sauce, 74
colored pastas, 16, 51–2
conchiglie, 16, 22, 28
    with roasted vegetables, 88
    stuffed shells, 92
conchiglie: con verdure
        arrostite, 88
    ripiene, 92
cooking pasta: combining
        sauce and pasta, 39

microwave, 36
pan, 32, 36–8
serving, 39
coralline, 23
cream, 63
    Alfredo's fettuccine, 69
    elicoidali with cheese
        and, 111
crème fraîche: spaghetti
        with eggs, bacon and
        cream, 110
creste di gallo, 25
culurgiones, 93

designer pastas, 24–5
ditali, 23
dolcelatte cheese, 62
dough: flavored and
        colored, 51–2
    making by food
        processor, 43
    making by hand, 42
    making stuffed
        pastas, 48–50
    rolling and cutting by
        hand, 43–5
    rolling and cutting by
        machine, 46–7, 53
dried pastas, 9, 12
    cooking, 36–7, 38
    flat, 20–1
    long, 12–15
    short, 16–19
    for soup, 23
    stuffed, 22
durum wheat, 8, 9

eating pasta, 40
egg pasta, 8–9, 9–10,
        12, 16, 42–3
eggplants, 59
eggs: spaghetti with eggs,
        bacon and
        cream, 110
    vermicelli omelette, 78
elbow macaroni, 17
eliche, 16, 28
elicoidali, 18
    with cheese and
        cream, 111
elicoidali di mezzanotte, 111
equipment: general
        cooking, 32–4
    pasta-making, 34–5

farfalle, 17, 23, 45
    with tuna, 79
farfalle: al sugo di
        tonno, 79
festonelle, 20–1
fettuccelle, 15, 26
fettuccine, 14, 15, 26, 47
    Alfredo's, 69
fettuccine all'Alfredo, 15, 69
fidelini, 15
fileia, 19
fiorelli, 25
fish, 58–9
    see also anchovies;
        salmon; shellfish; tuna
flat pastas, 20–1, 27
flavored pastas, 16,
        24–5, 51–2
fontina cheese, 62
    macaroni with four
        cheeses, 114
food processors, 43
frappe, 15
fregola, 23
fresh pastas, 26
    cooking, 37, 38
    long and flat, 26–8
    short shapes, 28–9
    stuffed shapes, 29–31
    see also dough
frittata de vermicelli, 78
funghetti, 23
funghi porcini see porcini
fusilli, 13, 16, 17, 28
    with ham and cheese, 118
    with tomato and
        balsamic vinegar
        sauce, 84
fusilli con salsa di pomodori
        all'aceto balsamico, 84

garganelli, 19, 28–9, 45
garlic, 60
gemelli, 19
gigli del gargano, 25
gnocchi sardi, 19
gomiti, 17
Gorgonzola cheese, 62
    macaroni with four
        cheeses, 114
    penne with chicken,
        broccoli and
        cheese, 75
gorzettoni, 22
Grana Padano cheese, 62
grano duro (durum wheat), 9
grattini, 23
gruyère cheese: fusilli with
    ham and cheese, 118
    macaroni with four
        cheeses, 114

ham: fusilli with ham and
    cheese, 118
    see also bacon; pancetta
heart disease, 10
herbs, 54–5
    flavored pasta, 51
    silhouette pasta, 53
homemade pasta, 42–53

lamb: lasagne with, 118
lasagne, 20–1, 27, 44, 47
    from Bologna, 115

with lamb, 118
mushroom and
    zucchini, 120–1
shellfish, 122
lasagne: ai funghi e
    zucchine, 120–1
    al ragù d'agnello, 118
    bolognesi, 115
    di mare, 122
lasagnette, 13, 20
lauro, 54
lingue de passera, 13
linguine, 13, 27
    with sun-dried tomato
        pesto, 85
linguine con pesto di

pomodori secchi, 85
lobster: capelli d'angelo
    with, 102
long pasta, 12–15,
    24–5, 26–8
lumache, 17
lumachine, 23
lumanconi, 17, 22

macaroni, 13, 17
    with four cheeses, 114
maccheroni, 8, 13, 17
maccheroni: ai quattro
    formaggi, 114
machines, pasta, 34, 35,
    46–7, 53
maggiorana see
    marjoram
malloreddus, 19
maltagliati, 45
manicotti, 22
marille, 25
marjoram, 54
    agnolotti with Taleggio
        and, 96
mascarpone cheese, 62
meat: cannelloni stuffed
    with, 116
    meat-filled agnolotti with
        vodka sauce, 70–1
    see also beef; ham;
        lamb; pork
medaglioni, 31
melanzane see eggplants
mentuccia see mint
microwave cooking of
    pasta, 36
millerighe, 18
mint, 54
    Sardinian ravioli, 93
mozzarella cheese, 62
    mushroom and zucchini
        lasagne, 120–1
    see also porcini
mussels: tagliolini with
    clams and, 103

nastroni, 15
nero di seppia see
    squid ink
noce moscata, 56
noodles, 44
nutmeg, 56
nutritional value of
    pasta, 10–11

occhi, 23
oils, 56–7
olio d'oliva see olive oil

olive oil, 56–7
olives, 58
omelette, vermicelli, 78
orecchiette, 19, 25
    with arugula, 89
orecchiette con la rucola, 89
orecchiettini, 23
oregano, 54
origano, 54
orzi, 23

paglia e fieno, 14, 28
pancetta, 58
    see also bacon: ham
panna da cucina
    see cream
pansotti, 30, 50
pantacce, 21
pappardelle, 15, 27, 44
Parmesan cheese, 62
    elicoidali with cheese
        and cream, 111
    macaroni with four
        cheeses, 114
    spaghetti and turkey in
        cheese sauce, 122
Parmesan graters, 34
Parmesan knives, 33
parsley, 54
pasta all'uovo, 8–9, 9–10,
    12, 16, 42–3
pasta cooking pots, 32
pasta corta, 16–19
pasta di semola di grano
    duro, 9
pasta integrale, 16
pasta lunga, 12–15
pasta machines, 34, 35,
    46–7, 53
pasta measurers, 33
pasta wheels, 35
pasta-making
    equipment, 34–5
pasticciata, 98
pasticcio di fusilli, 118
pastina, 23
Pecorino cheese, 62
    Sardinian ravioli, 93
penne, 18, 29
    with chicken, broccoli
        and cheese, 75
penne alla rusticana, 75

pennette, 18
pennini, 18
pepe see black pepper
peperini, 23
peperoncino see chiles
peperoni see peppers
pepper see black pepper
perciatelli, 13
pesto, 63
pie, pasta, 98
pine nuts, 58
pinoli, 58
pipe, 18
pizzoccheri, 19
pommarola, la, 68
pomodori see tomatoes
porcini, 60
    flavored pasta, 51
    mushroom and zucchini
        lasagne, 120–1
    rigatoni with wild
        mushrooms, 80
pork: cheese cappellacci
    with Bolognese
        sauce, 104–5
    ravioli with pork and
        turkey, 108–9
    see also bacon; ham;
        pancetta; sausage
potatoes: Sardinian
    ravioli, 93
poultry see chicken; turkey
prezzemolo, 54
primo piatto, 11
pumpkin, ravioli with, 106

quadretti and quadrettini, 23
quadrucci, 21, 44
quantities of pasta to
    serve, 11, 38
quills see penne

radiatori, 25
radicchio, 55
ragù: al vino rosso, 72
ravioli, 22, 30, 48
    with pork and
        turkey, 108–9
    with pumpkin, 106
    Sardinian, 93
    spinach and ricotta, 90–1
ravioli cutters, 35
ravioli trays, 35
ravioli: alla romagnola, 108–9
    con la zucca, 106
    di magro, 90–1
reginette, 13
renette, 23
ribbon noodles, 44
ricotta cheese, 63

elicoidali with cheese
and cream, 111
spinach and ricotta
ravioli, 90–1
stuffed pasta roll, 94–5
rigatoni, 18
with wild mushrooms, 80
with winter tomato
sauce, 83

*rigatoni: ai funghi de
bosco*, 80
*con sugo di pomodoro
invernale*, 83
risi, 23
rocchetti, 25
rosemary, 55
rosmarino, 55
rotelle, 18
rotellini, 23
*rotolo di pasta
farcita*, 94–5
rotondi, 30
rucola see arugula
ruote, 18

sacchetti and sacchettini, 31
saffron, 56
flavored pasta, 51
sage, 55
sale, 56
salt, 56
salvia, 55
sauces: combining with
pasta, 39
dressing up commercial, 63
matching to pastas, 40
scallops: shellfish lasagne, 122

seafood *see* fish; shellfish
semi di melone, 23
*semola di grano duro
e uova*, 10
semola flour, 9
serving pasta, 11, 39
shellfish, 59,
lasagne, 122
see also clams;
lobster; mussels;
scallops
short pastas, 16–19,
25, 28–9
shrimp: shellfish
lasagne, 122
silhouette pasta, 53
skillets, 32
soup pastas, 23, 44–5
spaccatella, 25
spaghetti, 8, 14, 24–5, 27
with eggs, bacon and
cream, 110
fresh tomato sauce, 68
and turkey in cheese
sauce, 122
spaghetti: alla carbonara, 110
tetrazzini, 122
spaghetti alla chitarra, 13, 47
spaghettini, 14, 27
spagliatelle, 24
spices, 56
spinach: flavored pasta, 51
and ricotta ravioli, 90–1
stuffed pasta roll, 94–5
squid ink, 59
flavored pasta, 51
stelline and stellette, 23
strangozzi, 25
strichetti, 17
striped pasta, 52
strozzapreti, 19
with zucchini
flowers, 81
*strozzapreti ai fiori di
zucca*, 81
stuffed pastas, 22, 29–31
cooking, 38
fillings, 48
making, 48–50

see also individual types
e.g ravioli
sugocasa sauce,
commercial, 63

tagliarini, 14, 28
tagliatelle, 8, 14, 24–5,
28, 47
three-color, 82
tagliatelle tricolore, 82
tagliolini, 14, 28
with clams and
mussels, 103
*tagliolini con vongole
e cozze*, 103
Taleggio: agnolotti with
Taleggio and
marjoram, 96
thyme, 55
timo, 55
tomatoes, 60–1,
cannelloni Sorrentina-
style, 124
flavored pasta, 51
fresh tomato sauce, 68
fusilli with tomato and
balsamic vinegar
sauce, 84

linguine with sun-dried
tomato pesto, 85
winter tomato sauce, 83
tongs, 33
tonnarelli, 13, 47
tonno see tuna
tortellini, 22, 31, 50
with ham, 72
tortellini con prosciutto, 72

tortelloni, 31, 50
trenette, 15
tricolore, 16
trofie, 19
trulli, 18
tubetti, 17, 23
tubettini, 23
tuffolini, 22
tuna, 59
farfalle with, 79
turkey: ravioli with pork
and, 108–9
spaghetti and turkey in
cheese sauce, 122

vegetables, 59–61,
conchiglie with roasted, 88
see also individual
vegetables
e.g. eggplants
vermicelli, 15
with clam sauce, 74
omelette, 78
vermicelli alla napoletana, 74
vinegar, 57
see also balsamic vinegar
vodka: meat-filled agnolotti
with vodka sauce, 70–1
vongole see clams
vongole sauce,
commercial, 63

wheat for pasta, 9
whole-wheat pasta, 16
wine: Bolognese sauce
with red, 72
to serve with
pasta, 41

zafferano see saffron
ziti, 15
zucchini flowers,
strozzapreti with, 81
zucchini: mushroom and
zucchini lasagne, 120–1
three-color tagliatelle, 82

Author's Acknowledgments

I am indebted most of all to Elisa Surini, for her invaluable assistance with this book, and also to Roberta Mitchell in Rome, for her up-to-the-minute knowledge and advice. I would also like to thank my daughter Sophie and the following, each of whom has given me some of her favorite recipes: Alessia Ferretti, Silvana Hobcraft-Capraro, Isabella Medri, Stefania Spiga and Karin Trczka. Last, but by no means least, I would like to thank Liz Mizon, for her unstinting administrative and technological support.

Publisher's Acknowledgments

The publishers would like to thank Jenni Fleetwood for her skilful editing, Annabel Ford for tracking down the pasta shapes for photography, photographers William Lingwood (recipes) and Janine Hosegood (cut-outs), props stylist Helen Trent, Lucy McKelvie and Kate Jay, who prepared the food for photography, Elisa Surini for checking the Italian terms, and Giuseppe Tranchina of Italbrokers Foodservice, who supplied egg pasta for recipe testing and photography.